PENGU[...]

AMERICAN BAGPI[...]

Iain Heggie was born in Glasgow in 1953. He le[...]
he was sixteen and had many jobs, including working [...]
instructor and drama teacher, before taking up full-time
writing. His first play was *A Wholly Healthy Glasgow* (1985),
which won a prize in the inaugural Mobil playwriting
competition. The first production was seen at the Royal
Exchange Theatre, Manchester, the Edinburgh Festival and
the Royal Court Theatre, London. *American Bagpipes* (1987)
was premièred at the Royal Exchange, while *Politics in the Park*
(1986) and *Waiting for Shuggie's Ma* (1986) have been
produced many times in Glasgow, Edinburgh, Manchester,
Liverpool and London. At present he is working on plays for
the Royal Court and the Tron Theatre, Glasgow.

  American Bagpipes won the John Whiting Award in 1987 and
the *Manchester Evening News* Best New Play Award in 1988.

IAIN HEGGIE

AMERICAN BAGPIPES
AND OTHER PLAYS

American Bagpipes
Waiting for Shuggie's Ma
Politics in the Park

PENGUIN BOOKS

PENGUIN BOOKS

Published by the Penguin Group
27 Wrights Lane, London W 8 5 T Z, England
Viking Penguin Inc., 40 West 23rd Street, New York, New York 10010, U S A
Penguin Books Australia Ltd, Ringwood, Victoria, Australia
Penguin Books Canada Ltd, 2801 John Street, Markham, Ontario, Canada L 3 R 1 B 4
Penguin Books (N Z) Ltd, 182–190 Wairau Road, Auckland 10, New Zealand

Penguin Books Ltd, Registered Offices: Harmondsworth, Middlesex, England

First published 1989
1 3 5 7 9 10 8 6 4 2

Made and printed in Great Britain by
Cox and Wyman Ltd, Reading, Berks
Filmset in Linotron Meridien by
Rowland Phototypesetting Ltd, Bury St Edmunds, Suffolk

Contents

Note on the Texts

Parentheses in dialogue signify

a) an abrupt redirection of a character's attention or intention:

SANDRA: Get back to receive a phone call. (What?)
(American Bagpipes, p. 5)

The first part of the line is self-expression for public consumption and needs no response. The second part is directly addressed to another character and demands a reply.

(b) a line or part of a line that is self-expressive but not intended to be heard:

SANDRA: (And what a carpet.) Oh I know you were.
(American Bagpipes, p. 6)

American Bagpipes

Characters

RENA NAULDIE Fifties
SANDRA MICHIGAN Her married daughter, thirties
WILLIE NAULDIE Her husband, fifties
PATRICK NAULDIE Her son, late twenties

Setting

The living-room of the Nauldie home. Four exits. A pale-blue
carpet, in functional carpet-tile squares. Worn but not ludi-
crous, and at the start of the play freshly cleaned. A couple of
gaps at the side of the carpet with a matching floor-covering.
Stains and worn patches should be arranged in preparation
to be concealed by furniture.

American Bagpipes was first performed at the Royal Exchange
Theatre, Manchester, on 4 February 1988 with the following
cast:

RENA NAULDIE	*Eileen Nicholas*
SANDRA MICHIGAN	*Eliza Langland*
WILLIE NAULDIE	*Campbell Morrison*
PATRICK NAULDIE	*Tom Mannion*

Director: Casper Wrede
Designer: Geoff Rose

Act One

Lights come up on room stripped of furniture except two pairs of straight-backed chairs stacked at the edge of the carpet. Clean, ironed police shirt on one stack of chairs, phone on the other, with cup of tea on the floor beside it. Enter SANDRA *from the street, in a coat and carrying parcels.*

SANDRA: [*As she enters*] Well that taxi definitely came a long way round, Mother.

RENA: [*Off*] Och the roads have all changed, Sandra.

[SANDRA *marches thoughtlessly on to the carpet.*]

SANDRA: And I told the man we were *in a hurry.*

[*Enter* RENA *with a coat on, carrying parcels, struggling a little more than* SANDRA.]

RENA: *Your father says* the roads have all changed.

SANDRA: And I told the man I had to *get back.*

RENA: Oh yes: the roads have all changed since you were last in Scotland. (Sandra!)

SANDRA: Get back to receive a phone call. (What?)

[*She drops her parcels in the middle of the floor.*]

RENA: The carpet, Sandra.

[*Pause.*]

SANDRA: Och the carpet'll be dry.

[*She throws off her shoes and tries the carpet with her feet.*]

RENA: *Your father's* carpet.

SANDRA: It *is* dry.

RENA: So I hope it's dry.

[*At the edge of the carpet still, she slips off her shoes and tries the carpet with her feet.*]

SANDRA: 'Your father's carpet.'
RENA: Because I was up half of last night –
SANDRA: (And what a carpet.) Oh I know you were.
RENA: Up half of last night *cleaning it* –
SANDRA: So don't you bother cleaning *anything else* –
RENA: Just because *you're* visiting.
SANDRA: Just because *I'm* visiting.

[*Pause.* RENA *is now satisfied, puts her shoes on and makes to cross the carpet to another exit but she begins to see the room.*]

RENA: Oh and look: your father hasn't left for his work yet.
SANDRA: Aye well I wish he –
RENA: Shirt *still* there since I ironed it.
SANDRA: I wish he –
RENA: Cup of tea lying cold. Likely.
SANDRA: I wish he'd hurry up and leave for his work, Mother.
RENA: So let's get this shopping junk *away.*

[*She continues towards exit.* SANDRA *crosses to pick up a chair, not picking up her share of the parcels.*]

SANDRA: Because I want peace, quiet and *privacy* to receive this phone call.
RENA: Because I don't want your father finding a mess.

[*Pause.* SANDRA *puts the phone on the floor and picks up a chair.*]

SANDRA: Well I think my father'll let me get into the place.
RENA: See: you don't –

[SANDRA *crosses with the chair and sits.*]

SANDRA: Let me put my feet up five minutes –
RENA: You don't –
SANDRA: I've been out trekking round buying presents for my family from Scotland.
RENA: You – Presents from Scotland for your family?

SANDRA: Yes.
RENA: What about presents from America for your mother?
SANDRA: I —

[*They stare at each other.* RENA *turns to go.* SANDRA *gets up.*]

RENA: No, you just don't *understand* —
SANDRA: Well you shouldn't —
RENA: Because your father's awful moody when he's getting ready for his work. And —
SANDRA: You shouldn't have to —
RENA: Are you *still* going on about this phone call?
SANDRA: You shouldn't have to put up with my father —
RENA: I don't even know *who* it is that's phoning you.
SANDRA: So *let him* be moody. (What?)
RENA: So who *is it* that's phoning you?
SANDRA: Oh no one *you* need bother with.
RENA: So is this you keeping secrets —?
SANDRA: An old friend from way back you wouldn't remember.
RENA: Imagine keeping it a secret from your mother!

[*Pause.*]

SANDRA: So — A secret? Because some holiday this!
RENA: And did you have to keep *going on* to this taxi driver?
SANDRA: Some holiday this: no privacy.
RENA: Did you have to keep *going on* to the taxi driver about *American* taxis?
SANDRA: No freedom to move.
RENA: 'American taxis are —'
SANDRA: And it's 'Don't leave a mess in case of your father.'
RENA: 'American taxis are —'
SANDRA: Oh it's 'Don't speak your mind to taxi drivers.'
RENA: '*American* taxi drivers are so honest.'
SANDRA: Because in case you haven't noticed, Mother —
RENA: I was so embarrassed.
SANDRA: I speak my mind to *everybody*.

RENA: I was so – Oh I know: don't remind me!

[*Pause.*]

SANDRA: But you know: back home in Fraserburgh –

RENA: So stop speaking your mind about America!

SANDRA: Back home in Fraserburgh, *New Jersey* –

RENA: Imagine 'speaking your mind' about America *to your father*.

SANDRA: Because if *I* was back home in Fraserburgh, New Jersey, I'd have that vermin of a taxi driver *up before the courts*. (What?)

RENA: 'Speaking your mind' about America's only going to put your father's back up.

SANDRA: What about my father putting *my* back up? 'How's the colony developing?' he goes.

RENA: And you know who has to suffer –?

SANDRA: I'll 'colony' him. In fact, if *he* was in Fraserburgh, New Jersey, I'd have *him* up before the courts for being a dirty rotten asshole of a father.

RENA: You know who has to suffer *in the long run*?

SANDRA: An asshole of a father and a husband!

RENA: Me!

[*Pause.* SANDRA *picks up another chair.*]

SANDRA: Yes, exactly, Mother: you!

RENA: And keep your voice down.

SANDRA: So why *not* come back with me?

RENA: I don't want your father hearing you speak –

SANDRA: Aye. Just come back with me to Fraserburgh, New Jersey.

RENA: Speaking your mind about Am– Och I couldn't go back with you to Fraserburgh.

SANDRA: You know you'd be welcome.

RENA: Imagine *me* in Fraserburgh.

SANDRA: You know you'd be *popular*! So, Mother –

RENA: Fraserburgh, New Jersey. (What?)

SANDRA: Promise you'll think it over.

RENA: Oh I'll think it over.

SANDRA: Good.

RENA: Aye, I'll think it over if *you'll stop speaking your mind about America to your father.* Because, as I say –

SANDRA: I won't even *mention* America. (What?)

RENA: It's me that's to suffer –

SANDRA: Oh *I know:* it's *you* that's to suffer –

RENA: } In the long run.
SANDRA:

[RENA *moves to go.* SANDRA *crosses with the chair and offers it to* RENA.]

RENA: But do you –?

SANDRA: So sit on your ass.

RENA: Do you really think I'd be popular?

SANDRA: Take your coat off.

RENA: Of course, people always *have* said, 'It's her sense of humour has seen Rena Nauldie through.'

SANDRA: Relax.

RENA: So if I *ever did* go to Fraserburgh, New Jersey, to live, I dare say you'd be right –

SANDRA: Screw my father!

RENA: Because I dare say *I would* be popular. (What?)

SANDRA: *Screw* – In fact: where *is* my father?

RENA: He'll be in the bath.

SANDRA: Shouldn't he be going to his work?

RENA: He'll be in the bath, *getting ready* for his work.

[*Pause.*]

RENA: So if I –

SANDRA: And you'll be pleased to know I haven't got any stupid-looking carpets.

RENA: If I do – (What?)

SANDRA: Pale blue –

RENA: Och. I'm not bothered about the carpet.

SANDRA: Stains easily, and —
RENA: Your father got the carpet from his work.
SANDRA: And you never see —
RENA: They were chucking it: he goes, 'Waste not, want not.'
SANDRA: *I've* never seen —
RENA: He goes, 'That's high-quality carpet: give it a wash, be good as new.' I went, 'Tut.'
SANDRA: No, I've definitely never seen stupid-looking pale-blue carpets in America.
RENA: Eh? Och . . .

   [*Pause.* RENA *sits.*]

RENA: But do you really think I'd be popular in —?

   [SANDRA *sits.*]

SANDRA: I — Yes: so just come back with me —
RENA: In America! Because I'd hate to —
SANDRA: Yes, just come back to America with me. (What?)
RENA: Because I'd hate to be a burden.
SANDRA: You wouldn't be a burden, Mother.
RENA: I —
SANDRA: Because all my friends and relatives in Fraserburgh, New Jersey, are dying to meet you. Oh yes: they're dying to experience your sense of humour.
RENA: Oh ho-ho: that's nice.
SANDRA: So if you'll *definitely* be popular, is that you *definitely* coming to Fraserburgh, New Jersey?
RENA: Och I'd have to think it over.
SANDRA: So what's there to —?
RENA: Because let's face it: you are awful *dominant*, Sandra.
SANDRA: Aye: you wouldn't think twice about it if *Patrick* asked you. You —?
RENA: I — Patrick?
SANDRA: I am not dominant.
RENA: Don't bring up Patrick, please.
SANDRA: Aye, if *your son* wanted you to go to America, you'd go like a shot.

RENA: Please –

SANDRA: So – (Not that they'd ever let his type *into* America.) So: *wouldn't you*?

[*Pause.*]

Sorry.

RENA: Oh forget it.

SANDRA: I promised I wouldn't bring Patrick up.

RENA: I don't get upset any more.

SANDRA: So I won't –

RENA: I've made progress in that department.

SANDRA: I won't bring him up *again*.

RENA: I don't *get* reduced to tears.

SANDRA: I won't –

RENA: I don't –

SANDRA: I won't –

RENA: I don't –

WILLIE: [*Off*] Woman!

SANDRA: I –

[*Pause.*]

WILLIE: [*Off*] I say woman!

SANDRA: Well don't you answer him.

WILLIE: [*Off*] Heh woman . . . ! Heh Bridget!

SANDRA: Don't – Who's *Bridget*?

RENA: [*Shouts*] What is it?

SANDRA: He's not *still* calling you –

RENA: [*To* SANDRA] 'Bridget' is your father's idea of a joke.

WILLIE: [*Off*] Bring me in my clean shirt.

SANDRA: Bridget!

RENA: Oh I know!

SANDRA: Your name's Rena, Mother.

RENA: Pathetic, isn't it? [*Shouts*] Aye, coming. [*To* SANDRA] 'Bridget.'

[*She puts down her parcels and picks up the shirt.*]

SANDRA: Let him get his shirt himself.

WILLIE: [*Off*] Come on, Bridget!

RENA: 'Bridget.'

WILLIE: [*Off*] And bring me in my tea.

RENA: It's not even funny. (What?)

SANDRA: Let him —

RENA: No, Sandra!

WILLIE: [*Off*] I'll be late for my work.

RENA: [*Shouts*] Your tea'll be cold.

[*She tries it.*]

SANDRA: Why can't he get it himself?

RENA: [*Shouts*] It *is* cold.

SANDRA: But *why* —?

RENA: 'Why?' (Tut.) '*Why?*'

WILLIE: [*Off*] Oh typical!

RENA: Because I don't want him running around *topless*.

[*She puts the tea back down.*]

SANDRA: Pardon?

RENA: You seen his tits?

SANDRA: His *tits*? Have they gone all to pot?

RENA: They're falling to bits.

SANDRA: My father's tits?

RENA: Sandra: your father's tits are falling to bits.

SANDRA: Oh Mother: ha-ha.

RENA: What?

SANDRA: Oh-ho.

RENA: *What?*

SANDRA: You would be so popular in Fraserburgh, New Jersey. Ha-ha.

RENA: Och that was nothing. [*Shouts*] I'll make you more.

SANDRA: Ha-ha.

WILLIE: [*Off*] Aye, don't bother.

RENA: [*Shouts*] *Aye.*

WILLIE: [*Off*] Not enough time.

RENA: [*Shouts*] I –
WILLIE: [*Off*] Bridget.
RENA: [*Shouts*] I – [*Quietly*] 'Bridget.'

[*She moves to go.* SANDRA *stops laughing.*]

So you would *definitely* get a shock, Sandra.
SANDRA: I –
RENA: You'd get a shock if you saw your father's tits, all right.
SANDRA: Oh?
RENA: Because the last time you were in Scotland, your father's tits were still standing. Ho-ho.
SANDRA: Mother, you –
RENA: Ah-ha.
SANDRA: Ha-ha.

[*She continues laughing.* RENA *moves to go.* SANDRA *stops laughing.*]

Oh and Mother.

[RENA *stops.*]

Your grandchildren want to meet you.

[RENA *moves to go and stops again.*]

RENA: Then why didn't you bring them to Scotland with you?
SANDRA: I –
RENA: Did you *forget* them?

[*Exit. Pause.*]

[*Off*] And put those parcels *away*.

[*Pause.* SANDRA *goes to the parcels and picks them up. She moves towards exit. The phone rings. She drops the parcels and rushes to the phone, almost knocking over the cup of tea. She catches it in time.*]

[*Off*] Answer that phone, Sandra . . . Sandra!

[SANDRA *picks up the receiver.*]

Thanks.

SANDRA: Hello? . . . Oh my God, Patrick: it *is* you. I never thought you'd *actually* phone. So where are you? . . . You *can't* be at the motorway. I haven't even – . . . No! You can't come now. I haven't had time to *prepare* them . . . You've –? What do you mean you've *got to* –?

[*It is clear that* PATRICK *has hung up.* SANDRA *puts down the receiver.*]

[*Mutters*] You've got to come *now*?

[*Enter* RENA *without her coat.*]

[*Aloud*] Oh my –

RENA: Have you not cleared up for me yet?

[*Pause.*]

I *asked* you to clear up.

[*Pause.*]

So 'do a thing yourself', right enough. [*Picks up the parcels and* SANDRA's *coat. Tries to pick up the cup, but can't manage it.*] And I suppose that was this old friend of yours . . . ? I mean: I see you got off the line before your old mother could overhear.

[*Exit. Enter* WILLIE, *doing up his uniform.*]

WILLIE: [*Shouts*] And turn my hot water off, woman.
RENA: [*Off*] What?
WILLIE: [*Shouts*] Aye, I've had my bath now. So turn it –
RENA: [*Off*] Och I've already turned your hot-water heater off. ('*My* hot-water heater.')
WILLIE: [*Shouts*] Turn – Aye, well done, Bridget.
RENA: [*Off*] 'Bridget.'
WILLIE: Your mother can be awful careless with my hot water, Sandra.
RENA: [*Off*] It's not even funny.

WILLIE: I'm only a constable.

[*Pause.*]

So. You get all you wanted . . . ? Sandra?

SANDRA: Eh? Oh is this you –?

WILLIE: All you wanted *out shopping*?

SANDRA: Is this you on your way to work?

WILLIE: Because that's a surprise, isn't it?

SANDRA: Your way to *work*? (Pardon?)

WILLIE: Because I thought you'd have even better shops *in America*. [*Starts looking for case-book.*] (Like everything else.) [*Stops looking.*] You're very quiet.

SANDRA: Oh –

WILLIE: You've usually got something to say for America.

SANDRA: I –

WILLIE: American planes or American whiskey or – (American whiskey!) – or American hotels. I goes to you, 'Aye, away and stay in a hotel.' I goes, 'And good riddance.' You go, 'There's no American hotels in Scotland.' I go, 'There's a Holiday Inn at the airport.' You go, 'I'm not spending my holiday at the airport.' I go, 'Aye, that's your excuse.' Ha-ha. Aye, very good, Willie. 'That's your excuse.' Ha-ha. You all right, Sandra? [*Looks round vaguely.*] And if you'll take my advice, you'll stop going on about America to your mother. Otherwise your mother'll end up wanting to go to America. And you don't want that burden round you, do you? Because your mother's the type wouldn't know a cowboy from an Indian. Ha-ha. No. [*Looks round vaguely.*] Now have you seen my case-book? I was –

SANDRA: Dad!

WILLIE: I was going to do some work in it last night on my bureau, but I can't seem to –

SANDRA: *Dad!*

WILLIE: Can't seem to – (What?)

SANDRA: When did you stop advertising for Patrick to come home?

[*Pause.*]

Because –

WILLIE: Aye, I wondered when *that* would get brought up.

SANDRA: Because would you be happy to see him again?

WILLIE: So I hope you haven't brought Patrick up to your mother either. (Happy?) Because I stopped advertising for Patrick to come home years ago. (So *happy*? Don't make me –) Have you brought Patrick up to your mother?

SANDRA: Just once. I –

WILLIE: Because when your mother gets upset – Well don't!

SANDRA: I –

WILLIE: Because when your mother gets upset about Patrick, it's *me* that's to suffer –

SANDRA: Dad, surely you –

WILLIE: In the long run. (What?)

[*Pause.*]

SANDRA: You can't blame me for bringing Patrick up.

WILLIE: I gave Patrick his chance.

SANDRA: You can't *blame* me for hoping to see my brother again.

WILLIE: I advertised for years. I –

SANDRA: Can you?

WILLIE: I spent a fortune advertising.

SANDRA: Because it might be long enough before I'm back in Scotland. (What?)

WILLIE: I'm only a constable.

SANDRA: Oh I know, Dad. Sorry, I –

WILLIE: I'm – Well it's not your fault, for once. I mean: I have always gone in for speaking my mind. Aye: speaking my mind to that shower of crawlers over my head. Because honesty doesn't get you promoted to sergeant these days. Oh no. It's lies and flattery and changing your hairstyle every other week. Isn't it? Now where's my –? [*Looks round vaguely.*] And don't bring Patrick up to your mother. Because you know what she's like –

SANDRA: I know –

WILLIE: You know what she's like about Patrick.

SANDRA: I know –

WILLIE: She'd cross the Atlantic on a bike for Patrick.

SANDRA: Oh I *know*. So what would you do, Dad, if Patrick were ever to turn up . . . ? By chance?

WILLIE: I – Patrick?

SANDRA: Patrick.

WILLIE: I'd kick him out the door head first no son of mine.

SANDRA: I –

WILLIE: Wouldn't I?

SANDRA: I see.

[*Pause.*]

WILLIE: Now: my –

SANDRA: So do you *need* your case-book?

WILLIE: I –

SANDRA: Can you not just go without your case-book?

[*Enter* RENA.]

I mean: do you –

WILLIE: Oh yes, I must have my case-book.

SANDRA: Do you need it for work *immediately*?

RENA: Is that him going on about his case-book next?

WILLIE: I've got to go through my cases with Sergeant McIntyre, later on this – (What?)

RENA: You'll've left your case-book *at* work, likely.

WILLIE: Bridget! Aye, later on with Sergeant McIn –

SANDRA: We'll look for it.

WILLIE: I had it here!

SANDRA: Then if we found it we could phone you.

RENA: Aye we'll phone you.

WILLIE: So – So what is this?

RENA: We'll phone you if we find it. Get to your work.

WILLIE: Are you two trying to get rid of me?

RENA: Get to – Oh: 'Are you two trying to get rid of me?' *Of course* we're trying to get rid of you. Aye. We'll –

WILLIE: Out of my own home too. (What?)

RENA: We'll phone you if we find it.

WILLIE: And I should think so too.

RENA: We'll – What's that supposed to mean?

WILLIE: It was probably *you* that lost it . . . Bridget. [*Moves towards exit and thinks better of it.*] And if you find it – the pair of you – don't bother snooping in it. It's private *police* business. OK?

RENA: *Who'd* read your case-book?

WILLIE: OK?

SANDRA: OK, Dad.

RENA: Poor wee criminals getting beaten up.

WILLIE: OK? I says. (What?)

RENA: Aye. Getting beaten up in the back of your van.

WILLIE: It's people like you –

RENA: I've *read* about people like *you*.

WILLIE: People like you the police force of this country protects.

RENA: I feel sorry for them.

WILLIE: We protect you from the criminal element and where's –?

SANDRA: It's OK, Dad. We won't read your case-book.

WILLIE: Where's your gratitude?

RENA: Take a joke, Willie: we won't –

WILLIE: And I hope you *did* switch off my hot water –

RENA: We won't be reading your case-book.

WILLIE: Bridget.

[*He moves towards exit.*]

RENA: 'My hot-water heater.'

[*He thinks better of it.*]

WILLIE: Well *you've* never gone out and done a day's work in your life to pay for a hot-water heater, have you . . . ? Have you . . . ? And get my furniture back in here, Bridget. Ha-ha.

[*Exit to street.*]

RENA: Thanks for not getting provoked, Sandra. 'My hot-water heater.' 'My furniture.' 'Bridget.' When my name's Rena. So it's not even funny. 'Probably *me* that lost his case-book.' Have you ever —? His sense of humour always was pathetic. Wasn't it?

SANDRA: So you'll definitely have to come to America now.

RENA: 'Bridget.'

SANDRA: Won't you?

RENA: What?

SANDRA: Treatment like that is a disgrace.

RENA: Oh Sandra, that's nothing. Your father's changed for the better.

SANDRA: Oh?

RENA: You know how he used to get drunk and hit me?

SANDRA: Don't remind me. I've still not recovered from my —

RENA: Well he doesn't hit me any more.

SANDRA: I've still not recovered from my violent childhood.

RENA: Now he gets drunk and goes, 'Would you care to dance?'

SANDRA: My violent — Oh Mother. How could you dance with *him*?

RENA: He goes, 'Put that frock thing on.' And I'm the fly type, Sandra: I *do* it. [*Gestures.*] So a wee dance round the coffee-table, he's happy. Pathetic, isn't it?

SANDRA: That still doesn't forgive —

RENA: Besides, he goes into Patrick's room these days and has a good weep.

SANDRA: That still — What for?

RENA: Because I didn't used to go into Patrick's room: he probably thinks he can weep in private.

SANDRA: My *father*?

RENA: Be his guilty conscience likely.

SANDRA: You're imagining it.

RENA: Yes, I definitely feel sorry for his wee criminals.

SANDRA: So you should definitely just come to America because –
RENA: Definitely feel –
SANDRA: I don't think he's changed.
RENA: Sandra!
SANDRA: I saw the dirty aggression in his face. (What?)
RENA: The case-book. It'll be in Patrick's room.
SANDRA: Och –
RENA: Quick. Go and get it. I'll shout your father back.
SANDRA: He'll've –

[*Exit* RENA.]

He'll've gone!

[*Pause.*]

[*Shouts*] And you shouldn't be running after him like that.
RENA: [*Off*] I don't want him poking the – Och.
SANDRA: [*Shouts*] If you came to America, I wouldn't make you run after me.

[*Enter* RENA.]

RENA: Poking the nose while I bring his furniture back in.
SANDRA: Aye. If you came to –
RENA: He'd be going, 'Watch you don't mark my good furniture.'
SANDRA: If you – Mother!
RENA: 'And watch you don't –'
SANDRA: If my father comes back, we'll just have to –
RENA: He's gone.
SANDRA: To – What? Yes, but *if* my father comes back, we'll get rid of him. Won't we?
RENA: Sandra.
SANDRA: Won't – (What?)
RENA: I put your parcels away.
SANDRA: I – Thanks.

RENA: In your room.

SANDRA: Yes, thanks.

RENA: Beside some other parcels.

SANDRA: I – (What?)

RENA: So what are the other parcels?

SANDRA: Oh it's just more presents.

RENA: Not *more* presents for your family in America?

SANDRA: No!

RENA: Who are they for, then?

SANDRA: Mother. Don't –

RENA: When are we getting them?

SANDRA: Oh you – When I see fit to give you them, OK?

RENA: Sorry. I mean: you shouldn't have bothered.

SANDRA: Oh it's no –

RENA: Because I haven't even bought yours yet.

SANDRA: It's not – *You* don't need to.

RENA: And you can't go back to America without a bagful of presents from your mother.

SANDRA: *You* can't afford it.

RENA: I'll manage to afford a wee thing.

SANDRA: You haven't got a job. In fact –

[*She takes out some money.*]

RENA: My grandchildren!

[SANDRA *hands the money to* RENA.]

My son-in – Oh no, Sandra, I –

SANDRA: Take it.

RENA: Don't be aggravating.

SANDRA: You're my mother.

RENA: In fact: don't be so *dominant.*

SANDRA: You – Sorry: you're right. [*Puts the money away.*] Sorry.

[*Pause.*]

Listen, Mother, I –

RENA: What's wrong with you, Sandra?
SANDRA: I – Oh . . .
RENA: Because I hope you didn't start going on about Fraserburgh, New Jersey, to your father.
SANDRA: Mother!
RENA: Stirring up trouble.
SANDRA: *Mother!*
RENA: Causing me problems. (What?)
SANDRA: Patrick's coming home.

[*Pause.*]

RENA: When?
SANDRA: Now.
RENA: *Now?*
SANDRA: Right now!

[*Pause.*]

RENA: Well –
SANDRA: Patrick was –
RENA: I mean –
SANDRA: Patrick was –
RENA: *If* I'd been warned – (Now?)
SANDRA: Patrick was the phone call.
RENA: At one time in my life – (Right now?)
SANDRA: Patrick was the guy on the phone. (Sorry.)
RENA: I'd've got the hoover out, the soup on, a bed ready.
SANDRA: I should've warned you.
RENA: But *Patrick?*
SANDRA: I kept putting it off. (What?)
RENA: Because oh my God, Sandra: I'm *not even changed.*
SANDRA: Patrick won't –
RENA: Look at me.
SANDRA: Patrick won't – If you want to get changed, go –
RENA: OK.
SANDRA: Go and get changed. There's time.
RENA: Right, I –

SANDRA: Besides, getting changed is a great idea.
RENA: I – Oh that's not very –
SANDRA: Because look at you.
RENA: That's not very – I know. Look at me.
SANDRA: So go and get changed.
RENA: OK.

  [*Pause.*]

But where's Patrick been all these –? And how did *you* –?
I mean: oh my God, Sandra: is he all right?
SANDRA: He sounds –
RENA: Does he sound well?
SANDRA: He sounds –
RENA: I'm awful glad.
SANDRA: I –
RENA: But look at the state of –
SANDRA: So go, Mother.
RENA: The hellish state of me.
SANDRA: Go and get changed.
RENA: OK

  [*Pause.*]

But what's he –? And what are we –? And oh my God,
Sandra: what's your father going to say?
SANDRA: Mother! We'll – We'll send Patrick out before my
father comes back. But sorry I –
RENA: Yes, but why –?
SANDRA: Sorry I didn't warn you, Mother.
RENA: Why –?
SANDRA: I wasn't to know Patrick wouldn't leave me time to
prepare you. I wasn't to know Patrick would reply to my
advert and then follow up his reply with a phone call. Was
I? (What?)
RENA: Why didn't Patrick come back before?
SANDRA: I don't know, Mother.
RENA: And look at the state of me.

[*Doorbell. Pause.*]

Oh –

SANDRA: Go and get changed, Mother.

RENA: Oh –

SANDRA: Go and get changed, for Patrick.

RENA: OK.

[*Doorbell.*]

Oh but Sandra: what about your father's case-book, if he comes back?

SANDRA: Mother! Just get changed. Get changed, then pick the case-book up from Patrick's room. OK?

RENA: OK.

[*Pause.*]

SANDRA: Mother!

RENA: *OK!*

[*Exit.* SANDRA *watches her and goes towards exit. The phone rings. She stops, then goes towards the phone. Doorbell. She stops, then goes out quickly, while the phone continues to ring.*]

RENA: [*Off*] Sandra!

[*Pause.*]

Answer that.

[*Pause.*]

Answer that, Sandra.

[*Enter* SANDRA *quickly.*]

Sandra!

[SANDRA *picks up the receiver.*]

Thanks.

SANDRA: Hello . . . She's gone to look for your case-book . . .
In Patrick's old room.

[*Enter* PATRICK, *carrying a bag and wearing a new suit.*]

OK, Dad, OK . . . See you, then. [*Puts down the receiver.*]
Well . . . Patrick Nauldie, eh?
PATRICK: Yes.
SANDRA: Patrick Nauldie, *after all these years*?
PATRICK: Aye.
SANDRA: In fact: how many years *is it*?
PATRICK: Oh . . .

[*Pause.*]

SANDRA: Are you thinking of speaking?
PATRICK: Ah, I didn't expect –
SANDRA: Or do I *still* get to do all the work?
PATRICK: I'm surprised you're *alone.*
SANDRA: Oh –
PATRICK: Excuse me.
SANDRA: Your mother will be through.

[*Pause.*]

So –
PATRICK: And where's the father?
SANDRA: At work. He'll be –
PATRICK: Could I –?
SANDRA: He'll be back shortly.
PATRICK: Could I get in touch with him?
SANDRA: What? *Why?*
PATRICK: I –
SANDRA: It's so urgent?
PATRICK: It's necessary.
SANDRA: After all these years?
PATRICK: I need to speak to him.
SANDRA: I mean: sorry.
PATRICK: I mean: him *too.* (That's all.) *What?*

SANDRA: Sorry!
PATRICK: Pardon? Oh, but it's –
SANDRA: I didn't mean to –
PATRICK: It's all right, whatever –
SANDRA: I didn't want to sound –
PATRICK: Whatever!
SANDRA: Mean or –
PATRICK: It's understandable.
SANDRA: Or anything. (What?)
PATRICK: After all.
SANDRA: Ah yes. And he'll be back shortly to –
PATRICK: Good.
SANDRA: To –
PATRICK: Perfect!

[*Pause.*]

So –
SANDRA: Well!
PATRICK: The old house is certainly –
SANDRA: What?
PATRICK: Certainly –
SANDRA: Oh the carpet's just been –
PATRICK: Oh so it's just been –?
SANDRA: Cleaned *last night*, in fact.
PATRICK: Not for me, I hope. Ha-ha.
SANDRA: And we were *just about* to bring the furniture –
  (What?)
PATRICK: Ho-ho. And *some* carpet, eh?
SANDRA: Actually, Patrick: if anything –
PATRICK: *What* a carpet!
SANDRA: The carpet was cleaned for *me*!

[*Pause.*]

PATRICK: Aye. So how are –?
SANDRA: Oh fine, fine.
PATRICK: How are *things*?

SANDRA: Pretty much as I told you in the –
PATRICK: So America, eh?
SANDRA: In the –
PATRICK: And married to an American? What's he –?
SANDRA: In the letter. (What?)
PATRICK: What's he like?
SANDRA: Ronnie?
PATRICK: And I'm –
SANDRA: Oh you know –
PATRICK: *I'm* an uncle?
SANDRA: He's – Yes. (Ha.) Three times.
PATRICK: I – Three, eh? Well I've done well. (Three!) I mean: *you've* done well. So well done. (Ha.)
SANDRA: Yes. (Ha.)

  [*Pause.*]

PATRICK: But who would have thought it would be *you* would go to America?
SANDRA: *I know!*
PATRICK: When it was always *me* that talked about it?
SANDRA: Yes. What? Oh *that's* what you –
PATRICK: Oh I didn't mean –
SANDRA: That's what you *mean*?
PATRICK: I didn't mean that it was *my idea*. (To *go* to America.)
SANDRA: I just thought you meant that *I* was always the –
PATRICK: And that you *stole* my idea. Or –
SANDRA: The home-lover. (What?)
PATRICK: Or anything. And *anyway*: you can *have* it. (Ha.)
SANDRA: *What?* (Sorry.)
PATRICK: You can *have* the idea of going to America!
SANDRA: Oh. Oh?
PATRICK: Free of charge. (Ha.)
SANDRA: Thanks. (Ha.)

  [*Pause.*]

So . . . How about a . . . a kiss? (For your –)

[PATRICK *gives her a kiss*.]

For your sister . . . Thanks.
PATRICK: No problem.
SANDRA: It was very nice.
PATRICK: You're . . . welcome.

[*Pause.*]

SANDRA: Oh . . . Look, Patrick. I might as well come to the –
PATRICK: Oh? So there's a –?
SANDRA: To the point.
PATRICK: There's a *point*? I mean: I *recommend* you –
SANDRA: Yes. The real reason I – (What?)
PATRICK: I *recommend* you to come to the point.
SANDRA: What?
PATRICK: Whatever.

[*Pause.*]

So . . . You had a point?
SANDRA: What?
PATRICK: A *reason*. You had a –
SANDRA: OK . . . ! The reason I got in touch –
PATRICK: Look, Sandra: I'm *glad* you had a –
SANDRA: What?
PATRICK: I'm glad you had a reason, OK? (For getting in touch.)
SANDRA: *What?*
PATRICK: Whatever.

[*Pause.*]

SANDRA: OK. So things *aren't* any better round here.
PATRICK: Oh? You mean –
SANDRA: I mean: between *them*.
PATRICK: Well that doesn't surprise –
SANDRA: In fact: things are as bad as –

PATRICK: I'm not surprised.

SANDRA: Things are as bad as when you left. Oh, and by the way –

PATRICK: Even though I left a long time ago. (What?)

SANDRA: That *is* why you left, isn't it?

PATRICK: *What?*

SANDRA: Isn't it?

PATRICK: As I say: I left a long time ago.

SANDRA: So you didn't leave because things were bad?

PATRICK: I don't remember *having* a reason . . . for *leaving*.

[*Pause.*]

SANDRA: OK. It was a long –

PATRICK: And if I did –

SANDRA: It *was* a long time ago. (What?)

PATRICK: If I did have a reason, I don't remember it *now*.

SANDRA: OK.

PATRICK: Sorry.

SANDRA: *OK!*

[*Pause.*]

PATRICK: So things are still *bad*?

SANDRA: Yes.

PATRICK: (You were saying.)

SANDRA: Yes . . . Yes, *they are*. So I want to take Mother back to America with me.

[*Pause.*]

PATRICK: Permanently?

SANDRA: Yes.

PATRICK: 'Oh?'

SANDRA: He's not going to change.

PATRICK: Not going to *mellow*, eh?

SANDRA: No. It doesn't look like it. He –

PATRICK: Will she go?

SANDRA: He *still* humiliates her. (What?)

PATRICK: *Will she go?*

[*Pause.*]

SANDRA: That's where you come in.
PATRICK: Oh?
SANDRA: You know she'll do anything you say.
PATRICK: Still?
SANDRA: So I'd like – Yes. Still. In fact: more so. More than
    ever! So I'd like you to –
PATRICK: Sandra, I –
SANDRA: I want you to *make her* come.
PATRICK: I –
SANDRA: And, I've got to say, I think it's the least you can do.
PATRICK: I – Oh *the least?*
SANDRA: Yes, the least. Because I think half the reason she's
    stuck it out with him is because she's been waiting *for you to*
    come back.
PATRICK: I see.

[*Pause.*]

Well I –
SANDRA: *Will* you?
PATRICK: I don't know if I'll have time.
SANDRA: Oh? How –?
PATRICK: (Sorry.)
SANDRA: How –?
PATRICK: But that's how it is.
SANDRA: I mean: why?
PATRICK: If that's all right?
SANDRA: I mean: how long are you thinking of staying?

[*Pause.*]

PATRICK: Oh not –
SANDRA: How long?
PATRICK: Not long.
SANDRA: And why is –?

PATRICK: Oh –
SANDRA: You've only just arrived. (What?)
PATRICK: Well circumstances: you know.

[*Pause.*]

SANDRA: I see. Look, Patrick. Is there something –?
PATRICK: What?
SANDRA: You seem –
PATRICK: Me?
SANDRA: You've *changed*!

[*Pause.*]

OK. I mean: I suppose it's to be expected.
PATRICK: I suppose it's not surprising.
SANDRA: No.
PATRICK: It is ten years.
SANDRA: Is it ten?
PATRICK: Ten.
SANDRA: No it's not surprising you've changed.

[*Pause.*]

OK. Will you help?
PATRICK: If there's time.
SANDRA: OK. Will you help in *what time you've got?*
PATRICK: If I can, ah, I mean: in any way I can.
SANDRA: Thanks.
PATRICK: That's all right.

[*Pause.*]

SANDRA: Oh. And ah incidentally . . . ?
PATRICK: Yes?
SANDRA: How are you?
PATRICK: Well. (Ha.) I could ask you the same thing.
SANDRA: You could. (Ha.)
PATRICK: Will I bother? (Ha.)
SANDRA: What?

PATRICK: In that case.
SANDRA: *What?*
PATRICK: Will I *bother* to ask you how you are? (Ha.)
SANDRA: Oh Patrick –
PATRICK: What?
SANDRA: Please yourself!
PATRICK: Whatever!

[*Long pause.*]

Look, ah, Sandra: *will* they be long?
SANDRA: *She* won't.
PATRICK: And what about *him?*
SANDRA: Oh he won't either. (So he said.) But she *definitely* won't. [*Shouts*] Mother!
RENA: Aye, just coming, Sandra.
SANDRA: Your boy's here to see you.
RENA: [*Off*] Oh, ah, oh – Oh *aye.* (Ha.) Hello, son.
PATRICK: [*Shouts*] Hello, Mother.
RENA: Get Sandra to take your coat.
PATRICK: [*Shouts*] I haven't *got* a –
RENA: [*Off*] Put the kettle on.
PATRICK: [*Shouts*] That's all right, Mother.
RENA: [*Off*] I'll just be a minute.
PATRICK: [*Shouts*] I'm – [*To* SANDRA] not thirsty.

[*Pause.*]

SANDRA: So actually I don't see why –? I mean: why after all these years you can't stay longer than –
PATRICK: Ah: longer than –
SANDRA: I mean: have you enough *time* to make my mother come back to America with me?
PATRICK: Longer than –
SANDRA: Well you'll just *have to* have time. (What?)
PATRICK: *Did I say* how long I am staying?
SANDRA: I –
PATRICK: (Exactly?)

SANDRA: No, you didn't. (Exactly.) But it had better be *long enough*, because America is your mother's only escape route from this – this –

PATRICK: The *only* escape –?

SANDRA: This hell on earth. The –?

PATRICK: Escape *route*.

SANDRA: The only . . . *escape* . . . *route*!

[*Pause.*]

PATRICK: So, Sandra: what is it you want me to do to her?

SANDRA: I don't know.

PATRICK: I mean: will I –?

SANDRA: Just whatever it was you always did do to her.

PATRICK: Will I knock my father out and hijack her?

SANDRA: (She would do *anything* for you.) I –

PATRICK: Because I –

SANDRA: No! We have to avoid –

PATRICK: I don't remember *doing* anything.

SANDRA: Avoid *confrontations*.

PATRICK: (To her.)

SANDRA: And avoid –

PATRICK: Oh avoid –?

SANDRA: Avoid talking to *him* about it.

PATRICK: Why? I mean –

SANDRA: Just talk to her quietly *on her own*. (What?)

PATRICK: I mean: have you got anything *against* confrontations?

SANDRA: I – Are you kidding? With my temper?

PATRICK: Because personally, I –

SANDRA: No, the only reason I don't stick a –

PATRICK: I *like* confrontations.

SANDRA: Oh yes. I'd quite happily stick a knife in his chest. (You know me.) What?

PATRICK: But don't worry: only carefully planned confrontations.

SANDRA: But a confrontation might lead him to take it out on her *later*.

PATRICK: Where you assess the situation first.

SANDRA: Whereas if we can get her to make her mind up to come to America, I can stay on in Scotland till the visa comes through and escort her out the country. (What?)

PATRICK: Before moving into *attack* . . . You know?

[*Pause.*]

SANDRA: Well there won't be time for that, will there?

PATRICK: Oh –

SANDRA: So you'll just have to get down to it right away, OK?

PATRICK: I – OK.

SANDRA: Good.

[*Pause.*]

So do you still play?

PATRICK: Pardon?

SANDRA: Are you still the musical type?

PATRICK: Sandra?

SANDRA: 'Amazing Grace' on a Sunday morning.

PATRICK: Oh –

SANDRA: Too much. (Ha.)

PATRICK: Oh *aye*. (Ha.)

[*Pause.*]

SANDRA: So *do you* still play the bagpipes?

PATRICK: I –

SANDRA: *Do* you? (I bet –)

PATRICK: Well to be quite honest, Sandra –

SANDRA: I bet you do.

PATRICK: The bagpipes are not in much demand in the south of England.

SANDRA: Oh?

PATRICK: No, not at the moment.

SANDRA: Well you surprise me, Patrick . . . Because, see, back home in Fraserburgh, New Jersey, they're the height of fashion.

[*Pause.*]

PATRICK: Well I could take it up again.
SANDRA: I – Yes.
PATRICK: (I suppose.)
SANDRA: Because you were good.
PATRICK: I – Was I?
SANDRA: And I mean that.
PATRICK: Thank you.

[*Pause.*]

SANDRA: So you're in the south of –?
PATRICK: Ah –
SANDRA: I mean –
PATRICK: Yes, that's how I –
SANDRA: Well I just sort of *guessed* you'd be –
PATRICK: I *saw your ad* in the south of England.
SANDRA: I knew you'd be *there*. (What?)
PATRICK: *That's* how I saw it.
SANDRA: I –
PATRICK: Didn't I?
SANDRA: Yes. Because I knew if you were in America you'd have got in touch with us –
PATRICK: I – Us?
SANDRA: Somehow. (What?)
PATRICK: Who'd –?
SANDRA: With me and my –
PATRICK: Who's *us*?
SANDRA: Me and my –
PATRICK: I –
SANDRA: My – Your brother-in-law!
PATRICK: I – Oh!
SANDRA: Your nephews!

PATRICK: Of course.

[*Pause.*]

SANDRA: Wouldn't –?
PATRICK: So where's –?
SANDRA: Wouldn't you? (What?)
PATRICK: Where's my brother-in-law?
SANDRA: Oh –
PATRICK: Where's Ronnie?
SANDRA: I didn't bring Ronnie. (Ha.) Because I –
PATRICK: And where's my nephews?
SANDRA: I didn't bring *anybody*.
PATRICK: I – I see.

[*Pause.*]

SANDRA: I thought if I bring *them*, she'll get to see them and it'll be that bit harder for me to tempt her over there. And – And you don't blame me for that, do you? Because –
PATRICK: Oh no. Not at –
SANDRA: Because it was for her own good.
PATRICK: Not at all.
SANDRA: So you won't mention it?
PATRICK: I –
SANDRA: Because I just let her think I wanted a rest from being a wife and mother. That I wanted the chance to go out and pick up a guy or two. (Ha-ha.)
PATRICK: Which isn't true? (Ha-ha.)
SANDRA: Well to tell you the truth, I wouldn't mind.
PATRICK: No?
SANDRA: Actually, no . . . I wouldn't. Ha-ha.
PATRICK: I see.

[*Pause.*]

SANDRA: So. What's it like in the south of England?
PATRICK: It?
SANDRA: Yes. *It.* Actually what are taxi drivers like in the south of England?

PATRICK: Taxi drivers?

SANDRA: Because round here –

PATRICK: Are you thinking of picking up a taxi driver?

SANDRA: Round here – Are you kidding? Because round here taxi drivers are a thieving lot of –

PATRICK: Oh they're the same all over.

SANDRA: A thieving lot of – Ah excuse me: I'll have you know, in America taxi drivers are the kind of people you'd invite into your house.

PATRICK: Which you do whenever you want a rest from being a wife and mother?

SANDRA: Because American taxi drivers – You know, Patrick, you *have* changed.

PATRICK: I – In what way?

SANDRA: Of course you always were –

PATRICK: What?

SANDRA: Oh I don't know: difficult.

PATRICK: Was I?

SANDRA: Yes. Ah *no*: that's –

PATRICK: How interesting.

SANDRA: That's not it. (What?)

PATRICK: How interesting you make me sound.

SANDRA: *What?*

PATRICK: Whatever.

[*Pause.*]

SANDRA: So –

PATRICK: But – 'It?'

SANDRA: I? (What?)

PATRICK: What's not 'it'?

SANDRA: Pardon?

PATRICK: It's difficult, isn't it? What is 'it'?

SANDRA: I don't know.

PATRICK: Well maybe it's just the pressure.

SANDRA: What?

PATRICK: The pressure of being back home after so long.

SANDRA: I –
PATRICK: (You know.)
SANDRA: Oh *I know*.

[*Pause.*]

But I suppose it's just that you seem really – really –
PATRICK: Oh please don't –
SANDRA: Really – No, I just can't put my finger on it.
PATRICK: Don't worry.
SANDRA: What?
PATRICK: It'll come to you.
SANDRA: *What?*
PATRICK: Whatever.

[*Pause.*]

PATRICK: So, Sandra: I'm still not sure what you –
SANDRA: Patrick –
PATRICK: What you – (What?)
SANDRA: We both want her away from here, right?
PATRICK: Ah . . . yes.
SANDRA: So just give her *your blessing* to come back with me
    to America.
PATRICK: I –
SANDRA: That'll be enough.

[*Pause.*]

In fact –
PATRICK: But what's she –?
SANDRA: I tell you what, Patrick.
PATRICK: What's she going to *do* over there?
SANDRA: Give her this.

[*She produces the money she tried to give* RENA *earlier.*]

PATRICK: And where's she going to live? And – And *how's*
    she going to live?

[*She tries to give* PATRICK *the money.*]

SANDRA: I'll make sure she's all right for money, Patrick. Because ever since I packed my bags and left for America, I've had *plenty* of money. Oh yes: you see I've got a job at the Holiday Inn, in Fraserburgh, New Jersey. [*Again tries to give* PATRICK *the money.*] It's true. And I've been doing *overtime.* Because when I come back home to Scotland on holiday, I want to be *extravagant.*

[*She again tries to give* PATRICK *the money. This time he takes it and puts it in his bag.*]

PATRICK: And I say it's from you?

SANDRA: No ... Yes ... *Imply* it's from me. Can't you? I mean: imply there's plenty more where that came from ... in America.

PATRICK: I —

RENA: [*Off*] Are you ready for me?

[*Pause.*]

PATRICK: [*Shouts*] Ready, Mother.

RENA: [*Off*] Because I'm coming.

PATRICK: [*Shouts*] OK.

[*Pause.*]

SANDRA: Oh and Patrick, if your father comes back, you'll have to go in the other room.

PATRICK: But, Sandra: you know I want to —

SANDRA: He doesn't know you're here yet.

PATRICK: You know I —

SANDRA: You'll need to give us time to —

PATRICK: I hope you don't need a lot of time, Sandra. Because —

[*Enter* RENA.]

SANDRA: Are you in *that* much of a rush?

PATRICK: I —

RENA: Patrick Nauldie.

PATRICK: I – Mother!

  [*Pause.*]

RENA: Right, Patrick. We'll need to get *the arrangements* sorted
  out.
PATRICK: We will.
RENA: So how long are you staying?
PATRICK: Ah –
RENA: Not long probably. So –
PATRICK: We'll need to see!
RENA: I thought so: 'We'll need to see.' He hasn't changed.
  Has he, Sandra?
SANDRA: Oh –
RENA: He's still the evasive type.

  [*Pause.*]

  Anyway: I'll get your room ready as soon as –
PATRICK: Well you look nice, Mother.
RENA: When there's time. (What?)
PATRICK: You look nice.
RENA: I know I do.
PATRICK: Doesn't she, Sandra?
RENA: Your father bought it.
SANDRA: [*To* PATRICK] Yes. [*To* RENA] My *father*?
RENA: He got some –
SANDRA: God: and him only a constable.
RENA: He got some –
PATRICK: *Still* a constable?
RENA: He got some football-duty overtime last winter.
PATRICK: (Fuck.)
SANDRA: *Of course* he's still a constable
RENA: Patrick!
SANDRA: With *his* big mouth?
RENA: Sandra . . . ! Well *neither* of you have changed. Fully
  grown adults the pair of you. Fully grown adults and *still*
  cheeky.

[*Pause.*]

SANDRA: ⎫
PATRICK: ⎬ Sorry, Mother.

RENA: Oh . . .

[*Pause.*]

PATRICK: So do you think my father *will* be long?

SANDRA: He said he wouldn't be long, Patrick.

PATRICK: Because I –

SANDRA: He'll be back *soon*. OK? That was him that phoned up: he's going to drive past and – [*To* RENA] Did you find his case-book, Mother . . . ? Mother . . . ? What is it?

RENA: Oh . . . nothing. I – I haven't *looked* for his case-book yet!

SANDRA: That's all right, then . . . But what is it?

RENA: Nothing!

SANDRA: OK. (Tut.)

[*Pause, broken by sudden burst of sobbing from* RENA.]

SANDRA: Oh Mother. (See: I knew!) What's –?

RENA: [*Weeping*] I'm fine.

PATRICK: Is she, Sandra?

RENA: No, I *am* fine, Patrick. But –

SANDRA: Well what *is* it, Mother?

RENA: Aye, I was just thinking . . . That's the first time you two have been cheeky since I told you off for coming back late from the ice-rink.

SANDRA: I wasn't cheeky.

RENA: You were. Cheeky as –

[*She starts laughing.*]

SANDRA: What? Was I? Was I cheeky?

RENA: You said that I was an 'old square'.

[*The others join in.*]

PATRICK: Anyway, Mother: I'm glad you're so well.

RENA: Oh aye. I'm —
SANDRA: Och.
RENA: I'm *fine*. Not bad, you know.
SANDRA: Listen to her.
RENA: I can't complain.
SANDRA: When I think that I have just witnessed one of the most shocking humiliations!
RENA: No, really, Patrick. Things *are* much better these days.
SANDRA: And all over some hot water for his bath.
RENA: Your father doesn't approve of waste.
SANDRA: It was a shocking, humiliating *incident*!

[*Pause.*]

SANDRA: And see —
RENA: What's the matter with you, Sandra?
SANDRA: See —
RENA: You losing your —?
SANDRA: Because back home in America: no one is mean with their hot water.
RENA: I —

[*Pause.*]

SANDRA: So —
RENA: Well, Patrick —
SANDRA: So —
RENA: I can deal with your father *nowadays*.
SANDRA: Yes, but this case-book, Mother.
RENA: Take this afternoon —
PATRICK: I —
SANDRA: I'll go and get it.
RENA: Take this afternoon, Patrick —
PATRICK: The case-book?
SANDRA: I'll — Yes, the case-book!
RENA: This afternoon I said to Willie —
PATRICK: Does he still write his case-book?
RENA: This afternoon I — Every day.
PATRICK: I remember the case-book.

RENA: I —

PATRICK: I used to say, 'Daddy, tell me a story from your case-book.' He'd go, 'Away and play.' Ha-ha.

RENA: Ha-ha.

PATRICK: So I *still* don't know what he writes in it. What does he write in it?

RENA: I don't know. Reports?

PATRICK: I'd like to read that.

RENA: Be just a lot of tripe – Oh son: it's private!

SANDRA: Yes. It's private. So what are you –?

RENA: But don't bother, son –

SANDRA: Why are you *wasting your time* on his case-book?

RENA: It *will* be just a load of tripe about criminals.

[*Pause.*]

PATRICK: That sounds interesting.

SANDRA: Listen to him next.

RENA: I don't think so, son.

SANDRA: How come you're interested?

PATRICK: Because I'm a criminal.

[*Pause.*]

RENA: Oh Patrick –

SANDRA: Imagine –

RENA: You're terrible. (Ha.)

SANDRA: Imagine saying that.

RENA: Aye. I see you've developed a sense of humour too. (Ha-ha.)

PATRICK: No, really: I've spent the past seven years in prison. (More or less.) Because I'm a criminal.

[*Pause.*]

RENA: I'll just go out and make your tea, son.

SANDRA: No. *I'll* make the tea.

RENA: No, *I'll* – Och! And is there anything you want with it, son? A cake?

PATRICK: Oh, ah yes, actually, Mum –

RENA: A biscuit?

PATRICK: I'd love a hot bath.

[*Pause.*]

RENA: Of course, son.

SANDRA: And what do you want a hot bath for?

RENA: Of course.

PATRICK: The journey. (You know.)

RENA: I'll put the hot-water heater back on.

SANDRA: No, *I'll* – Have you got *time* for a bath?

RENA: Of course he's got time. [*To* SANDRA] What is the matter with you, Sandra? [*To* PATRICK] Haven't you, Patrick?

PATRICK: I –

SANDRA: Well my father won't like *that*.

RENA: Haven't – Garbage!

SANDRA: Wasting hot water!

PATRICK: How come a 'waste'?

SANDRA: And we don't want a confrontation.

RENA: *I'll* settle your father.

SANDRA: Do we, Patrick?

PATRICK: Thanks, Mum. For settling my father. That's good of her, Sandra. Isn't it? (What?)

SANDRA: Do we?

PATRICK: Whatever.

[*Pause.* SANDRA *moves to go.*]

RENA: Where are you going, Sandra Michigan?

SANDRA: Mother.

RENA: What?

SANDRA: *I'll* make the tea. *I'll* put the hot-water heater on. In fact: *I'll* find the case-book.

RENA: Oh Sandra –

SANDRA: *You* entertain Patrick with your sense of humour.

RENA: My –? Ho-ho. But are you sure you can manage?

SANDRA: Because – (Mother!) Because I know Patrick's got a lot to say to you before his bath. Haven't you, Patrick?

PATRICK: Oh —

[SANDRA *moves towards exit in sarcastic triumph and knocks over the tea, which spills on to the carpet.*]

SANDRA: See —
RENA: Oh Sandra: you've stained your father's carpet.
SANDRA: It was an accident.
RENA: And you know what he's like about his carpet.
SANDRA: I'll clean it up.
RENA: You know — No!

[*Exit* SANDRA *with the cup.*]

Och Sandra: you've had no experience of pale-blue carpets.
SANDRA: [*Off*] Yes, *exactly*, Mother.
RENA: I —
SANDRA: Because in America you *don't get* stupid-looking pale-blue carpets.

[RENA *goes over to investigate the stain.*]

RENA: And between you and me, Patrick: I think Sandra's missing her family. Because a hellish *moody* bitch since she arrived. And she'll never get that lifted. It's tea, Patrick. It stains. And I don't know *who* she takes it from. Oh — ha — unless it's from her father, of course.
PATRICK: Ha yes, Mother. Probably from my father!

[*They laugh together. Enter* SANDRA *with a cloth. They stop laughing.* SANDRA *starts work.*]

RENA: She's wasting her time, Patrick. You're wasting your time, Sandra. And there's some spare —
SANDRA: It won't move.
RENA: There's — I said that to you.
SANDRA: But imagine —
RENA: There's some *spare* carpet.
SANDRA: Imagine pale-blue carpets.
RENA: I'll have to go and get that.

[*She moves to go.*]

SANDRA: No.

RENA: One of these days you pair will —

SANDRA: I'll get it, Mother.

RENA: You'll stop causing me so much *work*. (What?)

[SANDRA *overtakes* RENA.]

SANDRA: I'll —

RENA: OK.

[*Exit* SANDRA.]

I'll put my old feet up. Ha-ha.

PATRICK: Ha-ha.

RENA: [*Shouts*] It's in the store cupboard.

SANDRA: [*Off*] I know.

RENA: [*Shouts*] And bring me the knife and the hammer.

SANDRA: [*Off*] I know!

RENA: [*Shouts*] And some carpet tacks. [*To* PATRICK] Ha-ha.

SANDRA: [*Off*] I know!

RENA: Ha-ha. See what I mean?

PATRICK: Ha-ha.

[*Pause.*]

RENA: Well, Patrick —

PATRICK: Well, Mother . . . ?

RENA: Well I suppose you'll *have to* tell me what you've been doing with yourself?

PATRICK: Ah . . . you mean the last ten years?

RENA: Yes: probably a —

PATRICK: Well . . . eh . . . oh . . .

RENA: Aye: probably a catalogue of enjoyments!

PATRICK: Me?

RENA: You! If I know you. Aye: probably too busy *enjoying yourself* to even *think* about your old mother. Aye! But I'll get the whole sordid story out of you *some day*. (If I don't read about it in a gutter newspaper first. Ha.)

PATRICK: Ha.

RENA: But I'm awful glad to see you again, Patrick. How are you, son?

PATRICK: Oh —

RENA: Well that'll have to wait for now, Patrick. Your father —

[*She moves to start adjusting the stained patch of carpet.*]

PATRICK: Oh, ah —

RENA: Your father's due back. (What?)

PATRICK: There is one thing I —

[*Enter* SANDRA *with a patch of carpet, tacks, knife and hammer. She puts them down beside* RENA *and goes back out.*]

So —

RENA: What's the matter with her?

PATRICK: So — With Sandra?

RENA: She's probably missing her — She's probably missing big Ronnie.

PATRICK: She — I don't think so, Mother.

RENA: Oh? And what makes you say that?

[PATRICK *smiles at her.*]

Patrick Nauldie! Have you —?

PATRICK: It's nothing.

RENA: Have you and your sister been talking behind your old mother's —?

PATRICK: It's just that —

RENA: Your old mother's —

PATRICK: Sandra came to Scotland to pick up a taxi driver.

RENA: Her old back. (Is that all?)

PATRICK: And she thought you wouldn't understand.

RENA: Sandra always was the slutty type.

PATRICK: She —

[RENA *goes to work on the carpet.*]

RENA: So what was it you wanted to tell me?

PATRICK: I —

RENA: (Because you can't shock me!)

PATRICK: You –

RENA: I am listening.

PATRICK: Well something's been on my conscience, Mother. (You know.)

RENA: Och. (Tut.) Your con –?

PATRICK: Yes. I just want you to know why I haven't been in touch.

RENA: Oh Patrick: no need to drag –

PATRICK: Because I'd hate *you* to take it *personally*.

RENA: That's all – (Personally?) All that's *forgotten*.

PATRICK: No, Mother. (Sorry.) My conscience *dictates* here –

RENA: Oh –

PATRICK: Yes, I have to say *the reason* I stayed away for ten years *was*: I was afraid I'd hit my father.

RENA: Oh Pat–

PATRICK: Yes, Mother!

RENA: Surely not!

PATRICK: I openly admit it. I was afraid I would hit my own father and – And *if* I did that, there might be unpleasant consequences for *you*.

RENA: Me? Och I –

PATRICK: And –

RENA: I –

PATRICK: [*Making* RENA *listen*] And I had the idea, Mother – crazy, I know – that if I waited long enough I wouldn't *want* to hit him any more. Well I waited and waited, but the feeling that I wanted to hit my father – I mean *really* hit my father – just wouldn't go away. And I suppose I was in despair about it. Yes. Well then I saw this advert. (Sandra's advert.) It said, 'Patrick Nauldie come home.' And seeing this had a real *effect* on me. (You know?) So I just sort of realized that there probably *never would* come a time when I wouldn't want to hit my father.

RENA: Oh Patrick? Never?

PATRICK: Never! (Like any guy, I suppose.) So I thought to myself, you'll just have to face up to it, Patrick. You'll probably want to hit your father *for ever*. So *that's* why I've come home. To see if I can be – just *be*, you know – in the same room as my father and *control* my desire to hit him. And with *your* help, Mother, I'm sure I can *win through*.

RENA: Och don't worry, son. I've *never* lost the 'desire' to hit your father.

PATRICK: Ha: Mother! And *you'd* probably make a better *job* of hitting him, by the sound of it.

RENA: Ha-ha. That's *quite* a sense of humour you've been developing, Patrick. (You've been through a lot of *pain*, son. Haven't you? Oh yes. A lot of pain, just like your old mother.) And I hope you didn't come just for your father, Patrick Nauldie! I mean: just to 'hit' or 'not hit' your father! Ha-ha.

PATRICK: Oh no, Mother, not at all. Because I've also got ideas for *you*.

RENA: Me. (Ha.)

RENA: *You*, Mother.

RENA: Well surely not.

PATRICK: Oh yes. But clear something up for me *first*.

RENA: Oh –

PATRICK: What's this about you going to America to live?

RENA: Me?

PATRICK: Going to Fraserburgh, New Jersey, to live, with Sandra?

RENA: Because what's that sister of yours been *saying*?

[PATRICK *shrugs*.]

Because I don't think I'll be going to America.

PATRICK: No?

RENA: No! Because that sister of yours is an awful dominant besom. And I would hate to lose my independence.

PATRICK: So you've *no* interest in America?

RENA: I – Well I wouldn't say I'd *no* interest.

PATRICK: Oh?

RENA: Apparently in Fraserburgh, New Jersey, I'd be very

popular. (Popularity's not to be sniffed at.) And. Well your sister's husband's a fine-looking big specimen. Big Ronnie. A lovely tan. An outgoing personality. Nice tie with a lovely shirt. I could just fancy the hunk. According to his photograph. But your sister'll have got him like that. [*Gestures.*] (You know.) Ha.

[*By now she has removed the old carpet and cut the new one into the right shape.*]

PATRICK: Ha.

RENA: So I don't think I'll bother with America.

PATRICK: No?

RENA: No. So – And you know, Patrick: I think our Sandra's getting *worse*. I mean: she knows I'm desperate to buy presents for my grandchildren. Presents I can't afford. And she dominated me by trying to give me the money for them. So I just said, 'No thanks.' Ha-ha.

PATRICK: Ha-ha.

RENA: Ha-ha. So out with it: this 'idea' you've got for your old mother.

PATRICK: Well, Mother: I just wondered if you'd like to try *separating*? Because I'm sure you'll agree 'the family' has just about had it. I mean: all this hypocritical *pairing off* has outlived its –

RENA: How would I manage?

PATRICK: Outlived its – Eh?

RENA: How would I manage *for money*?

PATRICK: Oh well –

RENA: Not that *he's* ever given me any, the –

PATRICK: Suppose the financial side was not going to present a problem, Mother.

RENA: The big pig. What do you mean, son?

PATRICK: Wouldn't you *like* to set up *independently*?

RENA: Oh Patrick . . . You don't mean *with you*, do you?

PATRICK: Oh, ah, no. Not *that*, Mother. That's –

RENA: Because try as I might, I would just *cramp your style* if I moved in with you. You'd be wanting to *enjoy yourself* all the time and I –

PATRICK: You *couldn't* move in with me, Mother.

RENA: I – Why couldn't I, Patrick?

PATRICK: Because I'm a criminal.

RENA: Patrick!

PATRICK: And criminals live in prison.

RENA: You're not *still* –?

PATRICK: And even if *you* chose to become a criminal, Mother –

RENA: Patrick Nauldie –

PATRICK: If *you* became a criminal, Mother, they'd send you to a *woman's* prison.

RENA: A –? Now that *is* the limit, Patrick Nauldie! And why *do* you keep going on about criminals?

PATRICK: I *told* you, Mother. I am one.

RENA: Well I can't work out *why* you keep repeating yourself. Because you'll have to learn the first rule of a sense of humour is not to hammer a joke to –

SANDRA: [*Off*] Hot water's on, tea's ready. How do you like it, Patrick?

PATRICK: Oh –

SANDRA: [*Off*] Oh my God . . . He's *here*.

[*Car horn is tooted.*]

RENA: And I haven't even –

[*Enter* SANDRA.]

SANDRA: And I haven't even gone for the case-book yet.

RENA: And I haven't even tacked back down his carpet yet.

SANDRA: He won't notice. He won't be here for –

[*She and* PATRICK *exchange a look.* RENA *fumbles with the carpet, which she is still trimming a little. Exit* SANDRA *with the stained carpet, hammer and tacks.* RENA *gives up on it, discovering the knife in her hand.*]

RENA: So, Patrick: what will we say to your father about you?

PATRICK: It's OK, Mother.

[*He moves towards exit.*]

RENA: Oh Patrick.

[*She hands him the knife.*]

PATRICK: And you'll call me as soon as he's *prepared* for me?

RENA: Oh yes, son. Of course, son. As soon as –

SANDRA: [*Off*] That's him getting out the van.

[*He puts the knife in his bag and moves to go. He sees something in the bag. He stops.*]

PATRICK: Mother.

[*He takes the money* SANDRA *gave him out of his bag and hands it to* RENA.]

RENA: Oh Patrick.

PATRICK: For your grandchildren's presents.

RENA: Patrick, son.

PATRICK: Please take it.

RENA: I – You're so *tactful.*

[*She takes the money.* PATRICK *moves to go.*]

PATRICK: And don't tell Sandra, OK?

RENA: [*Disappointed*] No?

PATRICK: No. Because you know what *families* are like.

RENA: I – Oh don't tell me!

[*Exit* PATRICK *as* SANDRA *enters.*]

SANDRA: So, Mother –

[*Pause.*]

Mother!

RENA: I – What, Sandra?

SANDRA: I'll get the case-book and we can send my father away, OK?

RENA: You – What about Patrick?

SANDRA: We're sending my father away.

RENA: He wants to –

SANDRA: Because we don't want to –
RENA: He wants to –
SANDRA: We're not risking *trouble*.
RENA: I –
SANDRA: Are we, Mother?
RENA: No. Because I know what you mean.
SANDRA: We'll just tell –
RENA: But what will we tell Patrick?
SANDRA: We'll tell him my father absolutely refused to wait.
RENA: Eh?
SANDRA: He was in a hurry.
RENA: Oh *aye*. A hurry to –

[SANDRA *moves towards exit. Enter* WILLIE.]

To get back out to *arrest more criminals*. Ha-ha.
WILLIE: Where's my case-book?
RENA: I –
SANDRA: I was just on my way to –
WILLIE: Have you not found it *yet*?
SANDRA: To –
WILLIE: And what have you pair been –?

[RENA *and* SANDRA *share a look.*]

RENA: I'll go –
SANDRA: *I'll* go and get it.
WILLIE: No.
RENA: It's no –
WILLIE: I'm in a hurry.
SANDRA: It's –
WILLIE: I've a cop out there *waiting*.
RENA: I –
WILLIE: I'll get it *myself*. [*Moves to go and thinks better of it.*]
Because I don't want any of you pair snooping.
SANDRA: I don't –
RENA: We don't snoop. So –
WILLIE: You – Och!

[*He again moves to go.*]

RENA: So watch what you're saying, boy. 'Snooping.' More of that and I'll take my independence back.

[SANDRA *finds this significant.*]

WILLIE: You?
SANDRA: Her!
RENA: Yes: any more and I'll – I'll *leave*.
WILLIE: *You?*
SANDRA: *Her!*
RENA: Then who'd iron your shirts?

[WILLIE *stops in his tracks.*]

WILLIE: Where would *you* –?
RENA: I've got a variety of opportunities available to me.
WILLIE: Och –
RENA: So watch your lip.
WILLIE: My lip? Ha. Aye, very good, Bridget. My lip. Ha-ha. My –? Heh wait a minute. [*To* SANDRA] Is this your work, America?
SANDRA: Me? I –
WILLIE: This 'variety of opportunities'?
SANDRA: You're going too –
WILLIE: Because more of that and you can stay in one of your hotels.
SANDRA: You just went too far.
RENA: Don't bother with him, Sandra.
SANDRA: And I might just go to a hotel.
RENA: He's a poor tormented wreck of a lonely person.
WILLIE: Lonely? Away and –
SANDRA: I'm an *employee* of the Holiday Inn in Fraserburgh, New Jersey.
RENA: So don't listen to him.
WILLIE: Away and don't talk shite, woman.
RENA: You can't afford a hotel, Sandra.
SANDRA: So if I went to the Holiday Inn –

WILLIE: I have got friends like –

RENA: Friends? Hah! Don't make me –

WILLIE: Aye! Friends coming out my –

RENA: Don't make me – Aye: friends coming out your *arse*!

SANDRA: So if I went to the Holiday Inn at the airport, I'd be entitled to a discount.

[*Pause.* WILLIE *moves to go.*]

RENA: So where did you say this case-book was?

WILLIE: You know where it is.

RENA: Remind me again.

WILLIE: In Patrick's –

RENA: [*In extra-loud voice*] In *Patrick's room*?

WILLIE: Aye. And out my way you foul-mouthed trollop.

RENA: [*In extra-loud voice*] What's it doing in *Patrick's room*?

WILLIE: You – You put it there when you cleaned my carpets in a disorganized fashion . . . Bridget.

[*He again moves to go.*]

RENA: 'Bridget.'

[*Enter* PATRICK *with the case-book and his bag.*]

PATRICK: Hello, Dad. Long time no see. Is *this* it?

[*He seems to offer* WILLIE *the case-book.* WILLIE *does not respond.* PATRICK *seems to withdraw the case-book.*]

RENA: Surprise! Surprise! (Ha-ha.)

[WILLIE *looks at* RENA, *then* SANDRA.]

PATRICK: This *is* it, isn't it?

WILLIE: Ah, OK –

SANDRA: Dad, we –

WILLIE: OK –?

RENA: Willie, we –

WILLIE: No explanations!

[*Pause.*]

RENA: I –

SANDRA: We –

WILLIE: *No explanations*, I said. Now: the case-book.

PATRICK: Ah. So it is it. Good.

WILLIE: The case-book!

PATRICK: I'd hate to think I'd made a mistake!

WILLIE: *The case-book*, I —

PATRICK: Because I'd hate to think I'd been reading *someone else's* case-book. And that —

WILLIE: Read —? You!

PATRICK: And —

WILLIE: You —

PATRICK: And *I said*: that I'd been reading it, *for nothing*.

[*Pause.*]

RENA: Oh Pat—

WILLIE: OK —

RENA: Patrick, son —

WILLIE: OK —

RENA: Your father's case-book's private.

WILLIE: Just hand it —

PATRICK: Oh, ah, sorry —

WILLIE: Hand it over!

PATRICK: Sorry . . . I can't.

[*Pause.*]

SANDRA: Look, Patrick: don't mess about.

PATRICK: Ah —

SANDRA: My dad's to get back to his work.

PATRICK: Oh —

SANDRA: There's a policeman waiting outside.

PATRICK: Sorry, Sandra.

RENA: Patrick.

PATRICK: No . . . ! Sorry, Mother.

[*Pause.*]

RENA: Well we *thought* it would be a good surprise, Willie.

WILLIE: I said, *no* —

PATRICK: Oh Dad —

WILLIE: No *more*. And don't 'Dad' me: the –

PATRICK: I'm disappointed you're not curious about me.

WILLIE: The case-book.

PATRICK: Because I've got lots of curiosity about *you*.

WILLIE: You –? . . . [*To* RENA *and* SANDRA] What –? . . .
What's been –?

RENA: Oh –

SANDRA: Ah –

PATRICK: But I *can't* give you your case-book, Dad.

WILLIE: You –?

PATRICK: I haven't had my hot bath yet . . . Have I, Mum?

RENA: Oh Pat–

PATRICK: Have I, Sandra?

SANDRA: You –

PATRICK: And the bath's the only place I'll get a decent *private*
read of your case-book. Isn't it, Dad?

WILLIE: Right –

RENA: Oh Sandra –

WILLIE: That's it.

SANDRA: What, Mother?

WILLIE: Because *no bath*. Because no –

RENA: What happened –?

WILLIE: No hot water of mine.

RENA: What happened to that cup of tea, Sandra?

WILLIE: And shut the mouth, you pair. I'm talking. Now –

PATRICK: Oh Dad –

WILLIE: And –

PATRICK: You –

WILLIE: Have you been in my case-book?

PATRICK: You'll never talk like that to my mother and sister
again, OK?

WILLIE: Jesus Christ, boy: what is this? I – I've got *my work*
to go to. I've never been – I've never had a day off work in
my – So just give me the –

PATRICK: Never?

RENA: Give your dad his –

PATRICK: Because there's always a – (Sorry, Mum.) Always a 'first for everything'.

WILLIE: Right. This is all a load of – If you don't give me my – I'll – I'll –

PATRICK: I don't think so, Dad. I don't think *you'll* whatever ever again.

WILLIE: OK. What –? [*To* RENA *and* SANDRA] Look: do you know what –? What's happened to my son?

RENA: Oh Willie, it's just a –

PATRICK: Son? Oh? I'm his 'son'?

RENA: I think it's just *a joke*.

PATRICK: Because use words like 'son', Dad, and –

RENA: Isn't it, Patrick?

PATRICK: And you might upset me . . . Oh I don't know, Mother. Ask Dad if he's joking. Are you joking, Dad?

WILLIE: Look, Patrick: can we talk about this later. Can we –?

PATRICK: I won't be able to wait till later, Dad.

WILLIE: I mean: please –

PATRICK: Will I, Sandra?

SANDRA: I –

WILLIE: Please just give me my –

PATRICK: Sorry but no. Sorry because you've got so much to answer for.

WILLIE: Eh?

PATRICK: Haven't you?

WILLIE: Och away you and –

PATRICK: So we'll just *have to* talk about it now.

WILLIE: Away –

PATRICK: Or right after my hot bath, that is.

WILLIE: Away – Heh: I said – [*To* RENA *and* SANDRA] You two: when I go back to work, no hot bath for him, OK? OK?

PATRICK: So many terrible things to answer for.

SANDRA: Hah wait a – What?

PATRICK: Hasn't he, Mum?

SANDRA: What do you mean, Patrick?

PATRICK: Hasn't he, Sandra?

SANDRA: Because I had a *much worse* childhood than you . . .
[*Pause.*]

RENA: Sandra Nauldie –

SANDRA: Because the fights were much more *violent* before
you were born.

RENA: Don't you dare talk like that about your childhood.

SANDRA: And the foul language a lot more *offensive.*

RENA: You're too cheeky. When I think of what I have
suffered for –

WILLIE: Suffered?

RENA: Suffered *for you*, Sandra Nauldie.

SANDRA: I didn't ask to be brought into the world.

RENA: Suffered for *you*, from *him.* (What?)

SANDRA: And until I met Ronnie, it wasn't *worth* being
brought into.

WILLIE: What's going on?

RENA: Oh wasn't it?

PATRICK: That's not what you told me, Sandra.

SANDRA: I –

PATRICK: Is it?

SANDRA: You –

WILLIE: You selfish load of –

RENA: And you, you big violent pig you. I –

PATRICK: Remember the taxi driver?

WILLIE: Selfish load of swine.

SANDRA: I –

WILLIE: The lot of you.

SANDRA: Have you still not worked out that I was joking,
Patrick?

WILLIE: When I think what it was like to be a constable on the
streets of – of –

SANDRA: What's the matter with you?

WILLIE: I waded through razor gangs on a *daily basis.*

RENA: I –

WILLIE: *Daily*: just to keep you all in *luxuries.*

[*Pause. Horn is tooted.*]

RENA: Oh. Right, Patrick, son.

WILLIE: Yes. Enough.

RENA: Give your dad his case-book now.

WILLIE: The case-book.

RENA: The joke's over.

WILLIE: My colleague is *waiting*. He's –

PATRICK: I don't think you've understood me, Dad. So if you'd like to just send your colleague away, I'll *explain*.

WILLIE: Are you ser –? *What?*

PATRICK: Just send your colleague away. Because you're not going back to work. Ever. Are you?

[*Pause.*]

RENA: Ha-ha.

WILLIE: OK –

RENA: Anyone feel like tea yet?

PATRICK: Not for –

WILLIE: *OK* –

PATRICK: Not for me. *You*, Dad?

WILLIE: I – You – Tea? – Wait a minute. [*To* SANDRA] What were you saying to me earlier? Because have you got something to do with him coming here? Aye, coming here without my *consent*?

SANDRA: I – You – Don't you –

PATRICK: Stop! I think I can set you all right here.

WILLIE: Oh? Good.

RENA: Aye, good, Patrick: tell him, son.

WILLIE: I – *What?*

PATRICK: There's nothing *macabre* or *underhand* about my presence here today, Dad. Oh no. Because, in a way, everybody, I've come home to *celebrate*.

[*Pause.*]

SANDRA: Look, Patrick. I know we've all got a lot to *complain* about. I mean: it's a tough old life, I know *that*. But is it really –?

PATRICK: Sandra, I —

SANDRA: Is it really worth *all this*?

PATRICK: All what, Sandra? Don't —

SANDRA: Because we'll all be getting away from here, soon. Won't we? So why don't you just give my dad his —

RENA: Oh I know. We're all leaving, so —

SANDRA: His —

WILLIE: Oh 'leaving'? And where might *you* be going, Bridget?

RENA: I'm — ('Bridget': tut.) I'm —

WILLIE: Because you *couldn't* —

RENA: I'm setting up on my own.

WILLIE: *You* couldn't leave.

[*Pause.* WILLIE *laughs.*]

SANDRA: What do you mean, Mother? [*To* PATRICK] Because I thought she — [*To* RENA] I thought you had — [*To* PATRICK] I thought she was coming to America. *With me.*

RENA: Me?

WILLIE: Aye, take her to America.

RENA: Where did you get that idea?

SANDRA: *Patrick!* What's —

WILLIE: Take her to the colony. Ha-ha.

PATRICK: Ha-ha.

[*Pause.*]

Ah sorry, Sandra. Mum just *doesn't seem* to want to go to America. Isn't that right, Mum?

RENA: Ah yes, Patrick.

PATRICK: I —

SANDRA: If she's not coming to America with me —

RENA: Because Patrick's —

SANDRA: Where is she going?

RENA: Patrick's buying his old mother a house.

[*Pause.* WILLIE *and* SANDRA *laugh.*]

Why are you laughing?

PATRICK: Yes, *why*? (She could be right –)

RENA: Don't you laugh at me.

PATRICK: For all you know.

RENA: So why *are* you laughing?

SANDRA: Because things like this just don't happen in Fraserburgh, New Jersey.

PATRICK: The bagpipe town?

WILLIE: Fraserburgh –? The –? Ha-ha. Aye, very good, Patrick. 'The bagpipe town.' Ha-ha.

PATRICK: I know what you mean, Sandra.

WILLIE: The bagpipe town. Ha-ha.

PATRICK: Ha-ha.

SANDRA: You –

[*Horn is tooted.*]

WILLIE: Right. That *is* the limit. Now. The –

PATRICK: Dad.

RENA: Willie!

PATRICK: There you go again!

RENA: Just do without your case-book for once.

WILLIE: I –

RENA: Save a lot of bother.

PATRICK: Trouble understanding me.

WILLIE: I'll trouble you: I –

[*He tries to take the case-book.* PATRICK *resists successfully.*]

RENA: Oh Patrick –

PATRICK: Uh-uh.

RENA: Patrick, son –

PATRICK: Don't try that again, Dad.

RENA: Yes. Because I think Patrick *means* it, Willie.

[WILLIE *and* PATRICK *stand apart.*]

But why –?

PATRICK: Good.

RENA: Why do you –?

PATRICK: So —
RENA: Why do you *have to* have the case-book, Willie?
PATRICK: The celebration!
RENA: Because what do you *write* in your case-book?
WILLIE: Aye, it's none of your —
PATRICK: The — Yes, Dad.
RENA: Because I'm only ignorant.
WILLIE: None of you are worth —
RENA: I thought it would be boring shite.
PATRICK: Tell everyone what you write in it.
WILLIE: And if I lose my job over this, I'll —
SANDRA: Patrick Nauldie: why —?
WILLIE: I'll —
PATRICK: Losing your job?
SANDRA: Why did you come here?
PATRICK: That sounds like a great idea.
SANDRA: Because —
PATRICK: Aye: lose your job.
SANDRA: Because —
PATRICK: We'll get on with the celebration.
SANDRA: Because did you come here to cause trouble?

[*Pause.*]

PATRICK: Mum, Dad, Sandra. (Sandra!) I —
SANDRA: I —
PATRICK: I'm being *published*!

[*Pause.*]

SANDRA: Patrick —
RENA: Patrick Nauldie: have you done something *wrong*?
SANDRA: That's absolutely fabulous.
RENA: What's 'published'?
SANDRA: It's fabulous, Mother.
RENA: I —
SANDRA: It means he's written a book.
RENA: *That's* why he's been too busy to write to his mother.

SANDRA: *That's* why he's been acting like a maniac.

WILLIE: Do you believe him?

SANDRA: Oh –

WILLIE: Because I don't believe him.

PATRICK: I –

WILLIE: Only decent people write books.

PATRICK: You –

[*Horn is tooted impatiently.*]

RENA: I –

WILLIE: And you never were the educated type.

SANDRA: You can't go back to work now, Dad.

WILLIE: Leaves school at sixteen. Runs away from home at eighteen.

SANDRA: Now you'll have to stay and celebrate.

WILLIE: Who'd publish you . . . ? The case-book.

SANDRA: Congratulations, Patrick. Oh and please: could I have an autographed copy?

PATRICK: Oh, ah –

SANDRA: They'll *love* that in Fraserburgh, New Jersey.

[*Horn is tooted impatiently.*]

PATRICK: Of course, Sandra.

SANDRA: Thanks . . . So will I go out and *speak* to that young cop, Dad? Will I go out and send him off?

WILLIE: You –

SANDRA: He's obviously getting impatient.

WILLIE: Don't you – Impatient? I'll 'impatient' him. He'll not be impatient with me. He can *wait*. He'll wait till I'm ready. These young cops. I'm ashamed of them, so I am. Enforcing the law of this country: unshaven, the trousers not pressed, and the hair all dyed *to buggery*. I – And that one out there's got *a degree*.

SANDRA: So what's the title, Patrick?

RENA: And what's it *about*, Patrick?

WILLIE: OK. If you've written a book, where is it?

PATRICK: I –

WILLIE: If you're getting published, show us a copy.

PATRICK: I —

WILLIE: And even if you have written a book, it — And if it *is* getting published, it just shows what a rotten stinking direction the world's going in.

RENA: But it might be a good story, Willie.

SANDRA: In fact: do you think I could have *two* signed copies?

PATRICK: Oh —

WILLIE: I'm going. And if you —

PATRICK: You don't seem happy for me, Dad.

WILLIE: If you so much as *open* my case-book, I'll — Happy? I —

RENA: Don't bother with him, Patrick. *We're* happy for you.

PATRICK: Thanks, Mum. But you know a boy likes to please his father.

WILLIE: Hah.

[*He moves to go.*]

PATRICK: No!

[*He blocks* WILLIE'*s way.*]

SANDRA: Just let him go, Patrick.

PATRICK: He's staying here because —

SANDRA: Because he's only an old misery that —

PATRICK: He's resigning.

SANDRA: That doesn't even like America. (What?)

PATRICK: He's resigning. From his job. As from now.

WILLIE: Ha. And why should I 'resign' on your —

PATRICK: I —

WILLIE: Resign on the say-so of a delinquent. Ha-ha.

PATRICK: Because — (Ha-ha.) Because I'm keeping you from now on.

WILLIE: I —

PATRICK: Oh yes. You kept me in *luxuries* for eighteen years. Now it's my turn to keep you.

WILLIE: I —

PATRICK: And don't think you have to feel obliged to me, Dad. I'm obliged *to you*. Because what would I have written

about without you? What would I have written about if
you hadn't done so many atrocious things to us all?

RENA: Well I hope you haven't written about your father,
Patrick. Because who's interested in *him*?

WILLIE: I – If you don't – If – I'll get that long-haired beatnik
out there to come in and –

RENA: Oh Willie: you can't arrest Patrick.

WILLIE: Who can't?

PATRICK: Don't worry, Mother. I don't mind being arrested.
I'm used to it. I'm a criminal.

[*Pause.*]

RENA: Ha-ha. Aye. See, Willie: I *told* you it was all a joke.

WILLIE: I –

PATRICK: Right. Well I'll go and have my bath.

WILLIE: I –

PATRICK: I'll go and lock myself in the bathroom and have a
damn good read of your case-book, Dad.

WILLIE: You –

PATRICK: Before you have me arrested.

[*As he moves to go,* WILLIE *makes another attempt to get the
case-book.* SANDRA *tries to intervene.* WILLIE *discovers his
clenched fist close to* SANDRA'*s face and restrains himself.*]

PATRICK: You won't try that again, Dad.

WILLIE: I'll call that cop in.

SANDRA: I –

PATRICK: And don't do that either.

WILLIE: I'll –

PATRICK: I controlled it, Mother.

WILLIE: I –

[RENA *bursts into tears as* WILLIE *and* PATRICK *stand apart.*]

Oh for fuck's sake –

SANDRA: You've gone too far.

PATRICK: Aren't you proud of me?

RENA: I'm just so pleased my son's turned out a success.

[*Pause. Exit* SANDRA *quickly.*]

WILLIE: I –

PATRICK: Thanks, Mum. So let's –

WILLIE: Success?

PATRICK: Let's – Yes, success. Let's carry on with the celebration. Let's open the presents.

WILLIE: I –

RENA: Oh Patrick. Have you bought your mother a present? Thanks very –

PATRICK: No, Mum.

RENA: Thanks very – No?

PATRICK: Sorry.

RENA: Well you might have bought your old mother a present after all these –

PATRICK: But Sandra did.

RENA: All these –

PATRICK: *Sandra* bought us all a present.

[*He goes into his bag and produces three presents. He gives one each to* WILLIE *and* RENA *and keeps the other.*]

RENA: Where's Sandra?

PATRICK: Open – She's getting your tea.

RENA: I don't want tea.

PATRICK: So open your presents, because –

RENA: What about Sandra?

PATRICK: Because I'm opening mine. [*Starts unwrapping.*] Sandra will want to contribute to the celebration.

RENA: You – I love presents.

[*She starts unwrapping.* PATRICK *finds a set of bagpipes covered in a check material that is clearly* not *tartan. Enter* SANDRA, *without tea.*]

RENA: Thanks for the present, Sandra.

SANDRA: Patrick Nauldie!

PATRICK: Are you all right, Dad? (What, Sandra?)

SANDRA: Mum, Dad. Don't open yours.

[RENA *stops unwrapping.*]

RENA: I –

SANDRA: Wait. Have you been in my room?
RENA: It's all right, Sandra.
PATRICK: Of course.
RENA: I haven't seen what it is.
PATRICK: I *always* go into people's rooms. I'm a criminal.

[SANDRA *makes some kind of attempt to re-wrap* RENA'S *present. She bursts volubly into tears.*]

It's all right, Sandra.
RENA: Patrick!
SANDRA: I was –
PATRICK: You'll get used to me being a criminal.
SANDRA: I was keeping them for my last day.

[*Pause.*]

PATRICK: This is *my* last day, Sandra.
SANDRA: Oh forget it.
PATRICK: I *had to* open it today.
SANDRA: It's too late.
PATRICK: And I think they're great.
SANDRA: The surprise is spoilt. (What?)
PATRICK: They're great. Thanks.
SANDRA: Oh – ha – it's nothing.
PATRICK: No, really. They're wonderful. What are they?
SANDRA: It's – They're bagpipes, of course.
PATRICK: They're not tartan.
SANDRA: They are tartan. That is tartan. It's American tartan.
It's *Fraserburgh, New Jersey,* tartan.
WILLIE: Ha.
SANDRA: They're American bagpipes.
WILLIE: Ha. The colony –
SANDRA: Just because *everything's* better in America.
WILLIE: The colony's got its own tartan.
SANDRA: But do you really like them, Patrick?
PATRICK: Yes, Sandra. I can't wait to try them out.
SANDRA: Oh ho-ho.
PATRICK: And sorry for spoiling your surprise.

SANDRA: Ho-ho. That's all right.

RENA: So can we open ours now?

SANDRA: Oh —

WILLIE: American bagpipes. Ha-ha.

PATRICK: I'm going for my bath. What are you doing, Willie?

WILLIE: Sergeant McIntyre. Sorry I'm late for work, but —

PATRICK: Willie?

WILLIE: My son's a criminal. Ha-ha.

PATRICK: Ha-ha. [*Moves to go with his bag and bagpipes. On his way he thinks better of it.*] Before you go back to work, Dad: maybe you'd like to have a look at this.

[*He produces a manuscript from his bag and hands it to* WILLIE. *Exit* PATRICK *with the case-book and bagpipes.* RENA *is unwrapping.*]

SANDRA: He's turned out a really amazing guy, our Patrick.

WILLIE: I provide for a household.

SANDRA: Hasn't he, Mum?

WILLIE: I protect the population.

SANDRA: In a hurry, he says —

WILLIE: I train up the young.

SANDRA: And still has time for his bath. Ha-ha.

WILLIE: To get kicked in the teeth. Kicked in the teeth. Kicked in the —

[*Exit.* RENA *and* SANDRA *share a look.* RENA *discovers a skirt in the same material as the bagpipes.*]

RENA: Oh Sandra, it's —

WILLIE: [*Off*] Where is he?

RENA: It's — Patrick's in the bath, Willie.

WILLIE: [*Off*] Because wait till I get hold of him.

[*Enter* WILLIE. RENA *starts opening his present.*]

These young cops: I'll have the — the *beatnik* removed from the force.

SANDRA: He'd had an emergency call.

WILLIE: I —

SANDRA: He said he'd call back for you later.

WILLIE: He —

SANDRA: And actually he seemed like a hell of a nice young guy. So is he?

[RENA *produces a jacket in the same material as the bagpipes and skirt.*]

WILLIE: I —

[RENA *holds the jacket up to* WILLIE. *He bursts volubly into tears.*]

SANDRA: Oh —

RENA: I told you —

SANDRA: I'm *really* sorry.

RENA: I told you —

SANDRA: He said he *had to* go.

RENA: I did tell you he'd changed for the better, Sandra. [*To* WILLIE] What's the matter with you? Do you not like it? [*To* SANDRA] Because it's going to look smashing on him. Isn't it, Sandra?

[WILLIE *bursts into tears again.*]

SANDRA: Oh Mother, what's —?

RENA: I've no sympathy for him. He's lonely. But that jacket's going to look —

WILLIE: I just want my family to be proud of me.

[*Long pause. Bagpipes warm-up noise from off.* SANDRA *picks up the manuscript.*]

SANDRA: Actually, you know, this looks quite interesting.

RENA: What's that, Sandra?

SANDRA: Patrick's book.

RENA: What's it called?

[SANDRA *flicks to the front.*]

SANDRA: Fa-mi-ly A-tro-ci-ties. Oh, 'Family Atrocities' by *Patrick Nauldie.*

[*'Scotland the Brave' on bagpipes from off.* RENA *and* SANDRA *look out as lights fade.*]

Act Two

Lights come up on empty stage. Straight-backed chairs and presents rearranged around a table. All necessary pieces of furniture that are not brought on during the act are now on. Enter RENA *and* WILLIE *from separate directions.* RENA, *wearing an apron, brings on an armchair.*

RENA: Some help in a minute.

WILLIE: So where's –?

RENA: Some help in with your bureau.

WILLIE: Where's –?

RENA: Because your bureau is that damned *heavy.*

WILLIE: Where's my bottle of whisky?

[*Pause.* RENA *arranges an armchair.*]

RENA: Oh God knows.

WILLIE: Because I – Oh typical.

RENA: God knows where your whisky is.

WILLIE: Typical of you to clean my carpet and –

RENA: You'll've *drunk* your whisky.

WILLIE: You'll've cleaned my carpet in a disorganized fashion and *lost* my whisky.

[*Pause.* RENA *rearranges the armchair.*]

RENA: Oh never mind your whisky.

WILLIE: Aye, you'll've lost my whisky.

RENA: Just help me in with your bureau.

WILLIE: You'll've lost my whisky de–

RENA: Because it's that damned *antiquated.* (What?)

WILLIE: You'll've lost my whisky *deliberately on purpose,* Bridget. Ha-ha.

[*Exit in one direction.*]

RENA: And what do you want your whisky for?

WILLIE: [*Off*] Ha-ha.
RENA: You've your work to go to . . . ('Bridget.')

[*Exit in another direction. Enter* PATRICK *from one direction, carrying his bag and bagpipes, and* SANDRA *from another, wearing her coat and carrying suitcases.*]

PATRICK: So, Sandra –
SANDRA: You bastard.
PATRICK: Thanks.
SANDRA: You hooligan.
PATRICK: I mean: thanks for the bagpipes. Great –
SANDRA: You *criminal.* (What?)
PATRICK: Great sound.
SANDRA: Oh don't –
PATRICK: Great *reproduction.* (Pardon?)
SANDRA: *Don't mention it!*

[*Pause.* SANDRA *puts down the cases.*]

PATRICK: So you're –?
SANDRA: I just can't stand it.
PATRICK: Obviously you're going somewhere.
SANDRA: I can't stand it here another minute.
PATRICK: Aren't you?
SANDRA: I know when I'm not wanted. (What?)
PATRICK: Because where are you going?
SANDRA: I'm getting the first flight home to America.
PATRICK: I see.

[*Pause.* PATRICK *puts down the bag and bagpipes.* SANDRA *moves to go.*]

I'm disappointed, Sandra.
SANDRA: I –
PATRICK: I had hopes for you.
SANDRA: You – Och!

[*She moves to go and thinks better of it.*]

PATRICK: Still!

SANDRA: But how could you?

PATRICK: Yes, hopes for you and me.

SANDRA: How could you write those things about me?

PATRICK: I thought we might discuss my book and –

SANDRA: How could you write those things about *them*?

PATRICK: And maybe even discuss changing your life. (What?)

SANDRA: I'll discuss nothing with you.

PATRICK: No?

SANDRA: No!

PATRICK: You didn't respond well to the truth?

SANDRA: I was shocked.

PATRICK: The truth can be shocking of course. Ha.

SANDRA: I was – Ha!

[*Again she moves to go and thinks better of it.*]

Oh and Patrick –

PATRICK: Sandra?

SANDRA: I'll take that money back now –

PATRICK: The money you –

SANDRA: The money I –

PATRICK: How do you know I –?

SANDRA: I gave you money for her.

PATRICK: I might have –

SANDRA: Come on! I'll –

PATRICK: I might have –

SANDRA: I'll need it to pay for my taxi. (What?)

PATRICK: What if I've already given it to –?

RENA: [*Off*] Patrick Nauldie!

PATRICK: To *her*!

SANDRA: I –

[*Exit in one direction. Enter* RENA, *with an armchair, from another.*]

RENA: Have you cleaned the bath out yet, Patrick?

PATRICK: Ah, *no*, Mum.

RENA: Because I hope you won't leave it to your old mother
to –

PATRICK: Ah, no, Mum, I –

[RENA *places the armchair.*]

I –

RENA: Oh and Patrick –

PATRICK: I – Yes, Mum?

RENA: Where's your father's case-book?

PATRICK: I –

[*He goes to his bag, takes the case-book out and gives it to*
RENA.]

PATRICK: So, Mum –

RENA: Thanks, son. Because –

PATRICK: How did *you* get on with my book?

RENA: I –

WILLIE: [*Off*] Bridget!

RENA: Oh –

[*Enter* WILLIE *from one direction. Exit* PATRICK *in another.*]

WILLIE: Where's my –?

RENA: Right, Willie Nauldie!

WILLIE: My –?

RENA: I hope that cop comes back for you shortly, because –

WILLIE: Have you not found my bottle of whisky yet? (What?)

RENA: Because *here*!

[*She offers* WILLIE *the case-book. He does not take it.*]

WILLIE: Ach, Bridget –

RENA: What's –? And when *will* this cop come back for you?

WILLIE: It's hardly *worth* going back to work.

RENA: When –? Well I hope you're not thinking of taking the
afternoon off, because –

WILLIE: It's – I'll take the afternoon off if I so choose.

RENA: Because you've never had a day off work *in your life*.
WILLIE: Because they're *all* at it these days. (What?)
RENA: Because you're the conscientious type.

[*Pause. She offers him the case-book again. He takes it.*]

WILLIE: Well roll on –
RENA: At least you –
WILLIE: Roll on my *first* afternoon off.
RENA: You –
WILLIE: The first of many! Ha-ha.
RENA: You used to be the conscientious type. (What?)
WILLIE: Where's Patrick?
RENA: I – He's cleaning out the –
WILLIE: Aye, where's my son till I congratulate him?
RENA: He's cleaning out the bath.
WILLIE: Till I congratulate him and apologize!
RENA: *For his mother*. (What?)
WILLIE: Till I apologize for not believing in him.
RENA: You don't even like your son.
WILLIE: Because if my son's turned out the educated type
    after all, he can read my case-book with –
RENA: You don't like your son using hot water.
WILLIE: He can read my – He can use as much of my hot
    water as he likes, because I'm celebrating.
RENA: You – Celebrating?
WILLIE: I'm celebrating my son's book.
RENA: I –
WILLIE: So where's my bottle of whisky . . . ? Bridget.

[*Exit in one direction, with case-book.*]

RENA: 'Bridget.' [*Shouts*] And don't you bother taking any
    more time off work, boy. Because until Patrick buys me
    this house, I've got to carry on living here. And I don't
    want *you* under my feet all day. Do I?
WILLIE: [*Off*] Bridget.

[RENA *moves towards a different exit.*]

RENA: Oh and Patrick?

[*Exit.*]

[*Off*] Patrick.

[*Enter* PATRICK.]

PATRICK: Yes, Mum?

RENA: [*Off*] And when you've finished cleaning the bath, son, could you come and give your old mother a hand to bring in his antiquated –

PATRICK: Yes, Mum.

RENA: [*Off*] His 'furniture'.

PATRICK: I –

RENA: [*Off*] Thanks, son. Because he's an old pig. *Isn't he?*

[*Enter* SANDRA *with more suitcases.* PATRICK *moves to go.*]

SANDRA: But how *could* you say those things about me?

PATRICK: I – Look, Sandra, exactly which –?

SANDRA: I mean: you wrote that *my own mother* doesn't –

PATRICK: *Which* bits offended you most? (What?)

SANDRA: You wrote that my own mother *doesn't trust me.*

[*Pause.*]

You –

PATRICK: She doesn't.

SANDRA: She – You wrote: 'My mother used to send me to deliver messages.'

PATRICK: She did.

SANDRA: She sent *me* to deliver messages *too.*

PATRICK: She sent me to deliver *special* messages.

SANDRA: Yes, I used to – *Special* messages?

PATRICK: She didn't trust you with them.

SANDRA: 'Special messages!' She – Why not? I mean: I was older and more –

PATRICK: So she *had* to send me.

SANDRA: I was more *responsible*. (What?)

PATRICK: But you were old enough to *understand and remember* the messages.

SANDRA: But I *wouldn't have* read the messages.

PATRICK: Which were private.

SANDRA: I wouldn't've – So what were these . . . 'private' messages?

PATRICK: Which – I don't know.

SANDRA: Because I definitely wouldn't've –

PATRICK: I – Look, Sandra, you –

SANDRA: I –

PATRICK: You've obviously *misread* my book.

SANDRA: I – (What?)

PATRICK: Otherwise you wouldn't've taken it *personally*.

SANDRA: I misread nothing.

PATRICK: Because *who* my mother sent to deliver messages *wasn't the point*. Who –

[*Enter* RENA *with a rug.*]

SANDRA: I –

RENA: Patrick Nauldie, you promised you – Sandra . . . Are you going somewhere?

SANDRA: I – Yes, Mother, I'm –

RENA: Because come and help me first.

SANDRA: I'm – So have you got a taxi number on you?

RENA: Come and – A taxi number?

SANDRA: Because I'm – Yes, a taxi number.

RENA: How would *I* know a taxi number?

SANDRA: I'm –

RENA: I can't afford taxis.

SANDRA: I'm – Yes, exactly, Mother. So just get your coat on and come back to America *with me*.

RENA: I – Are you going back to America?

SANDRA: Come – Yes. Thank God.

RENA: Well come and help me in with his bureau *before* you go back to America.

SANDRA: Thank — You mean you're not even going to try and stop me going back?

RENA: I — No . . . ! So come and help me. Yes, come and help me: because the telephone book will be *in* the bureau.

SANDRA: I —

[RENA *places the rug.*]

RENA: So come and help me . . . someone . . . ! Patrick?

PATRICK: OK, Mum.

[*Exit* RENA. PATRICK *moves towards exit.*]

SANDRA: I — And you wrote that you kept one of these special messages, Patrick Nauldie.

PATRICK: I —

SANDRA: You *kept* one you didn't deliver.

PATRICK: I — The woman refused it. She — Why?

SANDRA: You kept it and you've still got it. (What?)

PATRICK: The woman refused to accept it.

[*Pause.* PATRICK *moves to go.*]

SANDRA: So you kept it?

PATRICK: Yes.

SANDRA: You *actually* kept it.

PATRICK: My mother trusted me.

SANDRA: And you didn't give it back to your mother?

PATRICK: My mother — I was a child, Sandra. I was —

SANDRA: Show me the letter.

PATRICK: I was nine years old.

SANDRA: Show me it.

PATRICK: I was scared she would think I hadn't bothered to deliver it.

SANDRA: I —

PATRICK: And stop trusting me. (What?)

SANDRA: If there is a letter.

PATRICK: I —

SANDRA: Because if you don't show me it, how will I know it exists?

PATRICK: It's private.

SANDRA: In fact: how will I know anything in that book of yours exists?

PATRICK: It's — Oh 'fuck it', Sandra.

[*He takes a letter out of his bag. It is blank, faded and sealed. He gives it to her.*]

PATRICK: OK. Now —

SANDRA: But quite frankly, Patrick, I —

PATRICK: Pass it back.

SANDRA: Quite frankly I think we *should* open it.

PATRICK: Just pass — Why?

SANDRA: In case it's important.

PATRICK: I'm returning it to her *unopened*, Sandra.

SANDRA: In case it's important that we *destroy* it.

PATRICK: So as soon as we find the right moment, I'm returning it.

SANDRA: Maybe it's important she *forgets* about it. (What?)

PATRICK: I'm returning it, Sandra . . . Unopened.

[SANDRA *hands back the letter. He goes to put it in his bag, thinks better of it and puts it in his pocket.*]

SANDRA: Don't you dare, Patrick Nauldie.

PATRICK: I —

SANDRA: Don't you dare accuse me of deceit like that.

[PATRICK *takes the letter back out of his pocket and puts it in his bag.*]

Thank you.

PATRICK: Don't mention it!

[SANDRA *moves to go.*]

PATRICK: Oh and Sandra: do you know where my book is?

SANDRA: I —

PATRICK: And how did *they* get on with it?

SANDRA: It's totally unsuitable for them.

PATRICK: I —
SANDRA: I'm not having them read your book, Patrick.
PATRICK: You —
SANDRA: It would *kill* them.

[*Exit. Pause.*]

PATRICK: [*Shouts*] Sandra . . . ! What have you done with my book, Sandra? Because —

[*He looks quickly round the room, then starts to run after her.*]

WILLIE: [*Off*] What's my bottle of whisky doing *there*?
RENA: [*Off*] Will someone *please* —?
PATRICK: [*Shouts*] Sandra!
RENA: [*Off*] Is that you, Patrick?

[*Pause.*]

Patrick?
PATRICK: Fuck. [*Shouts*] Just coming, Mother.

[*He moves to go and thinks better of it. He takes the letter out of his bag and puts it in his shoe.*]

WILLIE: [*Off*] Was that you, Bridget? Imagine concealing my bottle of whisky in my gramophone. Aye, you're a — So I've a good mind to *arrest* you for that, Bridget.
RENA: [*Off*] Never mind your whisky. Just come and —
WILLIE: [*Off*] Bridget.

[PATRICK *opens one of* SANDRA's *cases and starts searching. Music comes on: 'Bimbo' by Jim Reeves.* PATRICK *snaps the case shut. Enter* RENA *with a coffee-table.*]

RENA: Who put that on?
PATRICK: I —
RENA: Because get that *off*, Willie. [*Drops the coffee-table.*] Because imagine playing your gramophone in the kitchen.

[*Exit.* PATRICK *goes into another case.* WILLIE *might be heard singing along provocatively from off. The presents for the family in America we saw earlier fall out with a little bag.* PATRICK *repacks the presents and closes the case. He is about to start searching another case when he sees the little bag. He picks it up and goes to repack it when something makes him look inside. He takes out a box of condoms. Suddenly the music stops. He moves to conceal the condoms.*]

WILLIE: [*Off*] Aw, Bridget!
RENA: [*Off*] Aye, never mind, Bridget.

[PATRICK *relaxes and looks at the box of condoms.*]

WILLIE: [*Off*] Brid-get!
PATRICK: New Jocks.
RENA: [*Off*] You've your work.
WILLIE: [*Off*] This is a celebration.
PATRICK: Strong but sensitive.
RENA: [*Off*] You've your work, I says.
PATRICK: Your ultra-safe prophylactic with –
RENA: [*Off*] Just help me in with your gramophone!
PATRICK: With contraceptive jelly.

[*He puts the box in his pocket and moves to go. He changes his mind and looks in another case. Enter* SANDRA *with more cases, unseen by* PATRICK. *She is about to speak when she thinks better of it and retreats. Music comes on again.* PATRICK *takes fright and snaps shut the case. Exit in the same direction as* RENA.]

RENA: [*Off*] Will you get that off, please?

[SANDRA *comes forward and puts down her cases.*]

WILLIE: [*Off*] Tell her we're celebrating, Patrick.

[*Music stops again.*]

RENA: [*Off*] You ready, Patrick, son . . . ? Lift!

[SANDRA *goes into one of the cases she has just brought in. She takes out* PATRICK*'s manuscript and looks round for some-where to hide it.*]

WILLIE: [*Off*] And mind you don't mark my good furniture, you pair.

RENA: [*Off*] I'll mark your arse if you don't stop –

WILLIE: [*Off*] Bridget.

RENA: [*Off*] And see this house you're buying me, Patrick? Can it have all built-in furniture and all dark-coloured carpets?

[SANDRA *quickly and efficiently finds the carpet patch. She puts the manuscript underneath it and rolls an armchair over it as* PATRICK *and* RENA *enter carrying the gramophone and* WILLIE *enters carrying the whisky, which he has evidently sipped.* SANDRA *retreats quickly to the phone. She picks up the receiver and dials.* WILLIE *carries in a table-lamp.*]

RENA: Because I'm sick to death of shifting his antiquated furniture every time I clean his antiquated carpets.

SANDRA: Directory Enquiries?

RENA: Who moved his armchair?

SANDRA: A *reliable* taxi firm, please.

RENA: Was that you, Sandra?

SANDRA: [*To others*] Sssssshhhh. I'm on the –

RENA: I'll sssshhh you. [*To* PATRICK] Just put it down, son.

SANDRA: [*Into the receiver*] *Any* taxi number, then?

WILLIE: And watch my gramophone, because –

[*They put the gramophone down.*]

SANDRA: I haven't got a name. So *any* name will –

WILLIE: That's high-quality gramophone.

SANDRA: [*To* WILLIE] Sssssshhh.

WILLIE: Heh –

SANDRA: [*Into the receiver*] *Any* name of *any* taxi will do.

[RENA *moves the armchair.*]

WILLIE: Heh America: watch the –

SANDRA: [*To* RENA] No, Mum. Not there. It doesn't go – [*Into the receiver*] What do you mean you're 'really supposed to be given a name'. You – See you *Scots*? You make me –
WILLIE: Watch the lip.
SANDRA: You make me sick.
RENA: What are you talking about, Sandra?

[RENA *and* PATRICK *lift the gramophone.*]

SANDRA: Oh forget it.

[*She puts down the receiver.*]

RENA: How long have I lived here for?
SANDRA: I –
WILLIE: I mean: at one point –
RENA: I know where his effing furniture goes.

[RENA *and* PATRICK *put the gramophone on a patch.*]

SANDRA: I –
WILLIE: At one point lip like that would have made me *aggressive*, America.
SANDRA: I'm sorry.
WILLIE: I – That's OK. Because you see, Patrick –
SANDRA: I don't know what I was thinking of.
WILLIE: You see, Patrick, son –
SANDRA: It must have been that stupid bitch made me – (What is it, Mum?)
WILLIE: You see, I'm a reformed character. Amn't I, Bridget?
SANDRA: Mum?
WILLIE: And that's why, Patrick, I've decided to forgive you.

[*Pause.*]

Oh yes. I forgive you for all you've done to us. I forgive you, and here's my case-book. [*Picks up the case-book and gives it to* PATRICK.] Read it till your heart's content, eh? I was just being cautious earlier. My training, you know? Ha-ha . . . What do you say, son?

[RENA *bursts into tears.*]

SANDRA: Oh Mother, I –

WILLIE: Aw, what's the matter now, Bridget?

RENA: That's the first time I've ever said a really bad word.

SANDRA: Ah –

WILLIE: Rubbish, woman.

SANDRA: You didn't actually *say* it, Mother.

WILLIE: You swear non-stop till –

SANDRA: You only said –

RENA: Don't you say it, Sandra.

WILLIE: You swear like a trollop.

RENA: I do not.

SANDRA: Oh Mother –

RENA: At least, I didn't before I met *you*.

SANDRA: Mother, you –

RENA: I never thought I'd say words like –

SANDRA: You've got to get out of here!

[*Pause.*]

PATRICK: Oh for fuck's sake.

RENA: Patrick –

PATRICK: Just cut this crap.

RENA: Patrick, son.

PATRICK: Just cut it, OK?

RENA: I didn't know *you* swore.

PATRICK: OK?

[*Pause.*]

OK. So –

SANDRA: I don't believe this.

PATRICK: So –

SANDRA: I mean –

PATRICK: You're all going to have to start listening to each other.

SANDRA: I – What right have you got to tell us what to do?

[*Pause.*]

You –

WILLIE: Every right.

SANDRA: You – Ah: excuse me –

WILLIE: Because he's the educated type.

SANDRA: I'm a happily married –

PATRICK: Ha.

SANDRA: I'm a – (Ha? Ha to you)

WILLIE: And because he's –

SANDRA: I'm a happily married citizen of America. ('Ha.')

WILLIE: He's –

SANDRA: No one tells me what to do.

WILLIE: He's written a book.

[*Pause.*]

PATRICK: You –

WILLIE: So will you all realize that –

PATRICK: You haven't even *read* my book, Dad.

WILLIE: That –

PATRICK: And neither have you, Mum.

WILLIE: This is a celebration.

PATRICK: Because Sandra stopped you.

[*Pause.* WILLIE *takes a drink and goes to the gramophone.*]

RENA: I beg your pardon, Patrick Nauldie.

WILLIE: Eh no, son.

SANDRA: I stopped them reading it all right.

RENA: She didn't stop *me* reading it.

SANDRA: I read four and a half pages of this book.

RENA: I just didn't fancy it.

PATRICK: You –?

WILLIE: I – Your mother never was the educated type, Patrick.

PATRICK: Four and a half pages?

WILLIE: But then again, son, neither am I. Ha-ha.

SANDRA: I – I read four and a half pages, Patrick Nauldie, and every single word is totally unsuitable for them.

RENA: And let's face it, Patrick, you always did write a load of shite.

SANDRA: Four and a half pages of –

PATRICK: Four and a half pages wasn't enough to –

SANDRA: And see those four and a half pages?

PATRICK: It couldn't have been enough to –

SANDRA: It was four and a half pages *too bloody many*.

WILLIE: Ha-ha.

PATRICK: So no wonder you took my book *personally*.

SANDRA: I – Yes, no wonder. Because you wrote that –

PATRICK: What about the wider argument?

SANDRA: You wrote that –

PATRICK: The argument against family life.

SANDRA: I – Yes, you wrote that *I'm* a sadist.

PATRICK: The –

[*Pause.*]

RENA: So you are, Sandra.

SANDRA: And he wrote that I was like a –

WILLIE: Aye, well done, Patrick.

SANDRA: He wrote that the family had made me a –

WILLIE: This book sounds good. Ha-ha.

[*He is drinking. He plugs in the gramophone and table-lamp.*]

SANDRA: A –

RENA: At one point I thought I'd have to take you for *treatment*.

SANDRA: A frustrated, caged *animal*.

[WILLIE *selects a record.*]

RENA: Because do you remember the time I lent Patrick your bike one afternoon when he was only four and you were at school?

SANDRA: I was not a – Yes, I do. Because that's in his book as well!

RENA: And then you got the afternoon off because of the teachers' strike?

SANDRA: That was *my* bike.

RENA: And you chased after him with your skipping-ropes to get your bike back?

SANDRA: So I chased after him all right.

RENA: And you *whipped* him.

SANDRA: I —

RENA: Didn't she, Patrick?

PATRICK: I —

SANDRA: If I did whip him —

RENA: Didn't she, Patrick?

PATRICK: I —

SANDRA: If I *did* whip him —

RENA: That *was* sadistic, Sandra.

SANDRA: *If I did* whip him, it *just shows* what a nice person I am to be so concerned with my young brother's safety in case he accidentally rode my bike down the wrong side of the —

PATRICK: If you'd read my book properly —

SANDRA: It just shows that no matter what I do I'll never be as popular as Patrick.

PATRICK: If only you'd read it, you'd know that —

SANDRA: And it just shows that the sooner I get to hell out of here the better.

PATRICK: None of that's *the point*.

[*Pause.*]

WILLIE: Exactly, son. So Jim Reeves, everybody?

PATRICK: I —

RENA: You're not playing records, Willie.

PATRICK: I —

WILLIE: Bridget.

RENA: When that cop gets back, you'll have to be ready.

WILLIE: I —

RENA: Oh yes. You'll need to be sober for going back to your work.

WILLIE: I'm not *going* back to my work.

RENA: Tell him Pat– What?

WILLIE: Bridget. Ha-ha.

RENA: What's that supposed to mean?

WILLIE: Apparently my son's offered to keep me.

RENA: I –

[*Pause.*]

WILLIE: Haven't you, son?

RENA: It's me Patrick's keeping.

WILLIE: Aye, he'll be keeping you on the breadline, Bridget.

RENA: Tell him, Patrick.

WILLIE: Because he'll be keeping me in the style to which I am – Aye, tell her, Patrick.

PATRICK: I –

WILLIE: I'm not proud.

RENA: Neither am I.

WILLIE: Ha-ha.

[*He goes to take a drink.* PATRICK *takes the whisky from him.*]

Eh? Oh *aye.*

RENA: Well done, Patrick.

WILLIE: Aye, help yourself, son.

PATRICK: Right –

WILLIE: I should have offered, but –

PATRICK: We'll have to find my book.

SANDRA: Oh for God's sake.

WILLIE: Bridget's planked the whisky glasses.

PATRICK: It's my only copy.

SANDRA: Where's this bureau?

PATRICK: Because if you don't read my book, how will you learn that *isolation really works*?

[*Pause.*]

RENA: We'll get the bureau in now.

WILLIE: I –

SANDRA: Right, Mum. I'll —

WILLIE: No.

SANDRA: I'll help you.

WILLIE: We're listening to Patrick.

SANDRA: I —

WILLIE: Come on, Patrick: educate us . . .

PATRICK: I —

SANDRA: Why should I listen to him dragging up the past?

WILLIE: He'll be wanting us to look back and learn, Sandra.

SANDRA: The past should be forgotten.

RENA: Maybe he wants us to look back and laugh, Sandra.

WILLIE: Tell them, Patrick.

RENA: Imagine me if I didn't.

WILLIE: Because you'll need to learn to show a bit of balance,
    Sandra. Take —

RENA: I'd be pathetic.

WILLIE: Take Jim Reeves. American, I know. But on the
    other hand, the man's a genius. No two —

SANDRA: I doubt if you'd like to read what he wrote.

WILLIE: No two ways about that.

SANDRA: What he wrote about you.

WILLIE: So you'd better find this book, America.

RENA: Aye, where's this book, Sandra? Till I *find out* what he
    wrote about his old mother. Ha-ha.

SANDRA: Because I certainly can't forgive what he wrote
    about *me*.

RENA: 'My mother was an old bag.' Probably. Ha-ha.

WILLIE: The book, America.

RENA: Ha-ha.

SANDRA: So when this book comes out, I'm —

WILLIE: Just because you can't take a bit of educated
    criticism!

SANDRA: I'm suing him and that's final. Where's this bureau?

[*Pause. She moves to go.*]

RENA: Sandra Michigan —

WILLIE: Aye, and you sue my son —

RENA: You can't sue Patrick.

WILLIE: So you sue my son —

RENA: Patrick's your wee brother.

WILLIE: So if you sue my son, America, I'll stand up in court and tell them every fat ugly word he wrote about you is true. Oh yes. I'll stand up in court and say I'm proud of my educated son. Because I'll stand up in court and flash my dick at the judge. Ha-ha. Right. Where's my son's book?

[*He starts opening* SANDRA's *cases.*]

SANDRA: I — Stop him.

[*She tries to restrain* WILLIE.]

RENA: Don't bother stopping him, Sandra.

SANDRA: I've got to get out of this —

RENA: He'll only get a search warrant.

SANDRA: This hell.

WILLIE: She'll have my son's book planked.

[*He moves on to the case from which* PATRICK *took the condoms.*]

SANDRA: I — No.

PATRICK: It's all right, Dad. [*Helps her restrain* WILLIE.] She wouldn't have hid it anywhere so *obvious.*

[*He takes* WILLIE *away and returns the whisky into his hand.* SANDRA *tends to her case.*]

WILLIE: Quite right, son.

RENA: I wish you'd all stop hindering me.

WILLIE: She's not worth it, is she?

RENA: As if I didn't have *enough* to do.

[*She rearranges the furniture.*]

WILLIE: Aye, *just as well* I'm a reformed character these days otherwise I'd've — I'd've —

PATRICK: Shut up.

WILLIE: I'd've – Eh? Aye, quite right, son. Have a drink now?

PATRICK: Shut your fat ugly drunken mouth.

WILLIE: I –

RENA: You tell him, son.

PATRICK: Because this is not a joke.

RENA: I know.

PATRICK: This is not a game. Oh no. This is not even a celebration any more. Because see you, 'Dad', you're a pathetic trapped *woman-hater*.

[*Pause.* RENA *finishes with the coffee-table.*]

SANDRA: Ha.

RENA: Well I –

WILLIE: There's no doubt about it.

RENA: I could have told you that, Patrick.

WILLIE: You're right about me.

PATRICK: So tell me something, Dad.

SANDRA: Ha-ha.

WILLIE: And I can take it, you two.

PATRICK: So just how many women –?

WILLIE: I'm a reformed character, so I can take the truth. (What?)

PATRICK: How many women are there in this city anyway?

RENA: I –

WILLIE: How many *women*?

PATRICK: Yes.

WILLIE: None, everybody. Ha-ha. The city without women.

PATRICK: Ha-ha?

WILLIE: Ha-ha.

PATRICK: Because your case-book didn't make me laugh, Dad.

WILLIE: My –

PATRICK: A very unfunny document, my father's case-book, everybody. Oh no. Because I searched my father's case-book and found: not one case involving a woman.

WILLIE: I —

PATRICK: No women burglars, Mum. No women drug pushers, Sandra. No women prostitutes. No women murderers. In fact, everybody, no women *criminals*.

WILLIE: Ha-ha.

PATRICK: I — Ha-ha? Ha-ha! So if the women criminals of this city are going to walk the streets and not get arrested, what's that but *sexual discrimination*?

[*Pause.*]

SANDRA: Mother!

WILLIE: Now —

SANDRA: Where's this bureau, Mother?

RENA: Oh —

WILLIE: Of course my experience of women was limited.

SANDRA: Where is it?

WILLIE: It took me thirty-odd years to learn about them.

RENA: Willie Nauldie: you —

WILLIE: Buy them a few trinkets, shut them up.

RENA: You know I've kept myself a secret.

WILLIE: Buy —

RENA: 'Trinkets.'

PATRICK: Exactly, Mother.

RENA: You know nothing about me. (What, son?)

PATRICK: You *had to*.

WILLIE: Och Bridget.

RENA: 'Trinkets.'

WILLIE: What's there to know? Ha-ha.

PATRICK: Exactly, Father.

WILLIE: What?

PATRICK: Exactly.

SANDRA: I'm just sick to death of being *ignored*.

[*Pause.*]

Sorry, but —

PATRICK: OK. You're not —

SANDRA: I saved up for this holiday.

PATRICK: None of you are –

SANDRA: I did overtime at the Holiday Inn for three months to pay for *this*.

PATRICK: No one's going to side-step the seriousness of this issue with *trivialities*.

[*Pause.*]

WILLIE: I'm listening to you, son.

SANDRA: I'll side-step anything I like.

WILLIE: Ha-ha.

RENA: There's a whole array of things you don't know about me, Willie Nauldie.

WILLIE: Bridget.

RENA: And there's a whole array of things I know about you too.

SANDRA: I'll – I can't stand this!

RENA: Things you don't know I know about you. Ha-ha.

WILLIE: [*Sings*] 'I love you because you understand, dear.'

SANDRA: This fighting is driving me –

PATRICK: Exactly, Sandra.

SANDRA: I'm slowly going out of my –

PATRICK: It's *the family* that's driving you mad.

[*Pause.*]

WILLIE: ⎫ [*Sings quietly underneath* PATRICK] 'Every little
        ⎬   thing I try to do.'
PATRICK: ⎭ And this man here. This father. This husband. His spirit has been driven mad: it's been so destroyed by incessant contact with women in *the family* he *avoids* the entire female sex at every possible *opportunity*.

RENA: He doesn't avoid me.

PATRICK: So –

RENA: I avoid him.

WILLIE: [*Sings*] 'You're always there to –'

PATRICK: Constable William Nauldie?

WILLIE: 'Lend a helping hand, dear.' That's me!

PATRICK: There's no prostitutes in your case-book because every time you walk down the street and see one quietly soliciting you walk *across* the street and turn the corner. To avoid her.

RENA: Och Patrick.

PATRICK: My father's a *degenerate*.

RENA: Your father walks down the street and sees a prostitute quietly soliciting, he goes [*in American accent*], 'You doing business, honey?' So he goes, 'Eff off, buster. You're ugly.' Ha-ha. 'Trinkets.'

WILLIE: Bridget.

SANDRA: [*Roaring with laughter*] Oh Mother.

WILLIE: Aye, trinkets, Bridget.

SANDRA: You would be seriously popular in Fraserburgh, New Jersey.

PATRICK: Someone please say something I can *respect*.

WILLIE: 'But most of all I love you 'cause you're you.' Ha-ha. Aye, every time I walk down the street, see a prostitute quietly soliciting, I will no longer go to myself, 'No, Willie, this is just some wee lassie from the sticks earning a pathetic living, don't see it.' I'll go, 'Heh bitch. Get in the van.' Ha-ha. Respect that, son, eh? Because see your respect, Patrick, I'd love it.

RENA: Willie Nauldie.

WILLIE: Ha-ha. I'd *love* it.

RENA: You've been a bad wicked pig all your life. You'll get no respect from my son. Will he, Patrick?

PATRICK: I —

WILLIE: Aye! And next time I walk in the station I will no longer go, 'No, Willie boy, cool it.' I'll go, 'Sergeant McIntyre. See your arsehole, Sergeant McIntyre; you can stuff your thankless fucking job right up it.' Ha-ha. [*Sings*] 'No matter what the world may say about me.'

[*Horn is tooted.*]

Aye. Ya –
RENA: Oh Patrick.

[*Horn is tooted.*]

WILLIE: Ya beauty, Sergeant McIntyre. Because –
RENA: Oh Sandra.
WILLIE: Because that time is *now*. [*Picks up the whisky and goes out. Sings, off*] 'I know your love will always see me through.'
SANDRA: And see in Fraserburgh, New Jersey –
PATRICK: OK, Sandra.
RENA: He can't hand in his notice.
SANDRA: Back home in Fraserburgh, New Jersey –
PATRICK: Back to square one, then.
RENA: He can't hand in his notice, I said.
PATRICK: Where's my book?
SANDRA: In Fraserburgh, New Jersey, you *don't get* prostitutes. (What?)
PATRICK: Where's my book, Sandra? Because why did you stop them from reading it? Because fuck you. [*Runs off towards* SANDRA's *bedroom. Off*] You know I'm in a hurry.
RENA: He definitely can't hand in his notice looking like a drunken bum.

[*Pause.*]

Can he?
SANDRA: So, Mother, you –?
RENA: Can he, Sandra? (What?)
SANDRA: Could you lend me some money, Mother?
RENA: I –
SANDRA: Because I'm down to traveller's cheques already.
RENA: You –
SANDRA: So I'll need some money to pay for a taxi.
RENA: I –

[*A few notes of a crazy tune on a motor horn from off.*]

How humiliating.

SANDRA: What the hell is *that*?

RENA: Because they'll all be going, 'Mrs Nauldie. We saw your husband, in his police uniform, drunk as a –'

[*A few more notes.*]

Well at least I can say we've *separated*.

SANDRA: I –

RENA: Yes, I'll just say to them, 'Willie Nauldie? Nothing to do with me.' (What is it, Sandra?)

SANDRA: I – Mother, I –

RENA: Because you know I'm penniless.

SANDRA: You –?

RENA: You know I've not even got money to pay for my grandchildren's presents.

SANDRA: I –

RENA: Because you made such a bloody awful job of trying to lend me the money.

SANDRA: I –

RENA: Didn't you? And. So what happened to the money you offered me if you're so short of money? See, Sandra, you always were all mouth. All mouth and tactless. That's you . . . Sandra? Sandra!

[SANDRA *bursts into tears.*]

Aw Sandra, darling. You know I'd lend – You know I'd give you the money if I –

SANDRA: Why is Patrick the favourite?

RENA: Not a penny to my name.

SANDRA: Why do you prefer Patrick to me?

RENA: I –

SANDRA: Why did you send Patrick *special messages*?

RENA: You – I did not.

SANDRA: You did, Mother.

RENA: I did –

SANDRA: Because Patrick wrote about it in his book.

[*Pause.*]

RENA: Oh Sandra.

[*She rummages for money.*]

SANDRA: Well I know for a fact you sent him –
RENA: Here, Sandra, take it.

[SANDRA *goes to* PATRICK's *bag and opens it.* RENA *offers her the money.*]

SANDRA: I know for a –
RENA: Take my last penny for your –

[SANDRA *rummages in* PATRICK's *bag, and takes the money absently.*]

SANDRA: I –
RENA: For your taxi – Sandra!

[SANDRA *produces a folder.*]

What's that, Sandra Nauldie?

[SANDRA *starts to flick through the letters in it.*]

Is that my Patrick's book? Because – Because hand it over.

[*She starts chasing* SANDRA, *trying to snatch it out of* SANDRA's *hand.* SANDRA *is trying to dodge* RENA *and read the letters at the same time.*]

Because the boy looked awful *hurt* when I told him I hadn't read it.
SANDRA: This isn't his –
RENA: Come on, Sandra –
SANDRA: It's his –
RENA: I –

[*Crazy tune from off again. Continuous.*]

SANDRA: His correspondence.

PATRICK: [*Off*] What's going on out there?

[SANDRA *returns the correspondence to* PATRICK's *bag and continues her search.*]

RENA: Oh don't worry, Patrick, son. Your father will just be dancing in the street like a – Sandra!

[SANDRA *is searching* PATRICK's *bag.*]

SANDRA: Where *is* it?
RENA: Aye, his 'colleague' will be sitting in the police car knocking back your father's whisky. I've –
SANDRA: His colleague?
RENA: I've –
SANDRA: Right, Mother.

[*She closes* PATRICK's *bag.*]

RENA: I've seen it all before. (What?)

[*Exit* SANDRA.]

SANDRA: [*Off*] I'm getting him in for you.
RENA: Oh please yourself.
PATRICK: [*Off*] I'll kill Sandra when I get her.
RENA: Your book's here, Patrick.

[*She goes into* PATRICK's *bag and removes the folder just as the horn reaches a peak and abruptly stops. Enter* PATRICK. *She hands him the folder, which he takes.*]

PATRICK: I – Aw, Mum, I –
RENA: Is that you happy now, son?
PATRICK: That's not my book.
RENA: I –
PATRICK: Where's Sandra?

[*He puts the folder down. Exit.*]

RENA: She's gone to get her father. But between you and me, I hope she fails. Ha-ha.

[*Enter* WILLIE, *without whisky.*]

I hope she sends him back to –You swine!

WILLIE: To *Bridget.*

RENA: How can I be expected to get everything *back to normal*?

WILLIE: 'Bobby,' I says to my colleague, 'come away in.'

RENA: How –? Och!

[*She moves to go.*]

WILLIE: We'll get the Jim Reeves on, the wife'll make us up a sandwich.

RENA: You – Aye, no more sandwiches.

WILLIE: 'A sandwich, Bridget.'

RENA: And no more friends.

WILLIE: But these 'boys': they're too damned *shy* to accept my *hospitality*.

RENA: Aye, and the drink wears off, Willie Nauldie. You go to your friends, 'Get to eff you dirty bee you.'

[WILLIE *lurches towards her.*]

WILLIE: Care for a dance, Bridget?

RENA: Only the *actual words*, *right out.*

[*She dodges past him. He swerves and heads towards the gramophone.*]

WILLIE: Balderdash.

[*At the gramophone he swerves again and lands seated with startling uprightness on an armchair.*]

RENA: And who is it that has to run after your friends and apologize? ('Balderdash?')

WILLIE: But care for a dance, Balderdash?

[RENA *moves towards exit.*]

RENA: But no more. ('Balderdash.')

[*She thinks better of it.* WILLIE *gets up and goes to the gramophone.*]

RENA: Where's Sandra?

[WILLIE *puts on a record. Enter* PATRICK.]

RENA: I – Right, Patrick –

[WILLIE *scratches the record noisily.*]

WILLIE: Whoops. Ha-ha. The human element. [*Dances round the room, studying the record for a scratch.*] Care for a dance, Jim? Care for a –
PATRICK: How can you put up with this, Mother?
RENA: I – Right, Patrick: help me in with his –
PATRICK: How can you?
RENA: Patrick!
PATRICK: I –

[*She leads* PATRICK *out.*]

WILLIE: Care for a –? No, Jim. You don't, do you? Fuck you, then. Fuck you. [*Snaps the record in two.*] Aye: and your father's bloody colleague also drove off with your father's bloody married Yankee daughter and your father's bloody whisky after refusing your father's bloody Scottish hospitality. Aye, and see you, Patrick? You weren't ever *normal.* Sexual discrimination? You didn't even like *fishing.* [*Drops the snapped record and swerves to the gramophone.*] Jim Reeves? I love you. Give me a kiss, son. Aye, give me a big kiss. [*Takes out another record, starts kissing it and puts it on the turntable.*] And as for you, Bridget Balderdash, you've got my house like a tip. No, my son never cared about me, doctor. All he cared about was his bagpipes. Bagpipes and more pocket-money. More pocket-money to pay for more bagpipes. Bagpipes coming out his Bridgets, doctor. Oh yes. And he didn't like fishing. But to tell the total truth, doctor, *neither did I.* Oh yes, doctor, definitely a bagpipes and nut case, he was. Ha-ha. Aye, very good, Willie; a bagpipes and nut case.

[*Enter* PATRICK *and* RENA, *carrying the bureau, which they place.* WILLIE *puts his arm across the turntable.*]

And to sum up, doctor: oh yes: balderdash coming out his bagpipes. Ha-ha. Ha –

[*The gramophone needle sticks.*]

Bridget!

RENA: Will you get your gramophone *seen to*?
WILLIE: Have you scratched my good record?

[PATRICK *goes over and gently pushes* WILLIE *to one side,* WILLIE *topples and falls with unexpected pizzazz. Just as we are expecting him to get back up, he does not.* PATRICK *has taken the record off and looks at it.*]

PATRICK: Nothing wrong with the record.
RENA: That's what I said, Patrick.
PATRICK: It must be the –
RENA: But look at the – Aye, look at the lump.

[PATRICK *starts to experiment with the gramophone.*]

Look at the soul. Of course, my father warned me: 'Rena Bain,' he said. 'On your own head be it.' Listen? I laughed in my father's face. But it wasn't the body. It was just I'd never met anyone before so totally unlovable. Ha.

[PATRICK *is by now testing the level of the floor around the gramophone with his feet.*]

PATRICK: The floor's not level.
RENA: Patrick, son.
PATRICK: I –
RENA: No, don't. *Don't!* [*Runs over to him, gesturing for silence. In intimate voice*] We've not fixed his carpet yet.
PATRICK: I –

[*He stops work. He and* RENA *slowly focus on* WILLIE. *They see that he is unconscious. They turn back and* PATRICK *gestures that he wants to tilt the gramophone to one side. They are about to start work when* PATRICK *suddenly stops.*]

No, Mother. I –

RENA: I –

PATRICK: Sorry, but that's it.

RENA: Patrick!

PATRICK: I'm not going to be quiet. So –

RENA: Sssssshhh.

PATRICK: So stand up to him.

RENA: I've got to live here, Patrick.

PATRICK: If you're separating, you might as well stand up to him.

RENA: I've got to.

PATRICK: I –

RENA: Until I get this money off you for my house.

PATRICK: If you're – Stop going on about this money. I mean –

RENA: I – Right, just forget it, Patrick. I can fix the carpet another day when he's not here. (What?)

PATRICK: Is the money all that matters to you?

RENA: I –

PATRICK: Is the money *for your house* all that matters to you?

RENA: What's that supposed to mean?

PATRICK: Because I want you to prove to me it doesn't matter.

RENA: I –

PATRICK: Prove it. Give me back the money I gave you earlier.

RENA: Patrick Nauldie: don't you dare talk to your mother like that.

PATRICK: I –

RENA: So stop keeping me back, please. I've got things to do! ('Money.')

[*Exit* RENA *in one direction as* SANDRA *enters from another.*]

PATRICK: Sorry.

RENA: [*Off*] I'll money you. ('Sorry.')

PATRICK: I didn't mean it, Mother. I – I – You can *keep the money*.

SANDRA: Is this what you're looking for, Patrick?

[*She produces the money.*]

PATRICK: I –

SANDRA: Take it.

[*He takes it blankly.* SANDRA *takes the whisky from her coat pocket and puts it in the bureau.*]

I've made alternative arrangements for my transport.

PATRICK: I –

[SANDRA *sees* WILLIE.]

SANDRA: What's happened to –?

PATRICK: She went off in a huff with me.

SANDRA: Not *her*. Him.

PATRICK: The book.

SANDRA: Yes, I've been thinking about your book.

PATRICK: Less bullshit. Hand it over.

SANDRA: I –

PATRICK: Because if you don't, Sandra, I'll – [*Produces the box of condoms.*] I'll show these to Mum and Dad.

SANDRA: I –

PATRICK: And don't pretend that doesn't cause you a problem. You were *frantic* when he attacked your case.

SANDRA: I didn't want him pawing my –

PATRICK: I saw you.

SANDRA: I'm ashamed of nothing.

PATRICK: Who said anything about shame?

[*Pause.*]

PATRICK: So –

SANDRA: You went into my case.

PATRICK: I'm a criminal. The —

SANDRA: You took my present from Scotland for Ronnie.

PATRICK: The book! And I'll give you back your present for Ronnie with —

[SANDRA *bursts into tears.*]

I — Oh no! Right, stop this.

SANDRA: Why am I being blamed?

PATRICK: That book was seven years of my life.

SANDRA: Why am I being blamed *again*?

PATRICK: All I wanted was for my parents and you to read my book.

SANDRA: Why am I being used? (What?)

PATRICK: To read my book and *change your lives*.

SANDRA: I mean: I'd be *quite happy* to read your book and change my life.

PATRICK: I —

SANDRA: So I don't know why you have to be so *horrible*. I mean; I think the bit about husbands and wives 'almost inevitably blocking what is best in each other' —

PATRICK: I —

SANDRA: Is absolutely *wonderful*.

PATRICK: Oh!

SANDRA: Because, Patrick Nauldie, I've found it so true to *my experience*. I've found it *so true*. I mean: when I got on that plane to America after you'd run away from home like a coward. Yes, when I got on that plane to America, there was no book, there was no person there to warn me that Ronnie might be sitting next to me. Oh no. There was no one there to warn me that if I married him when we got off the plane, he might deliberately block out what's best in me. That he would block what's best in me, after I'd had his children for him. No. And no one warned me that after I'd had his children for him I'd be too old to become an air hostess and travel. Because there was no one there to warn me that after I'd *had* his children I might start to *hate* them.

And after I'd had his children for him no one warned me that I might start pissing about buying stupid presents from Scotland for him because I had the crazy idea they'd perk up the lousy rotten sex life he gives me. So *that's* why I wanted to admit to you that *although* it's true I did find some bits of your book a bit *uncomfortable*, I was honestly—I was honestly *trying* to come round to them. So now what am I going to do? Because my father's colleague has offered me a lift and a phone number and to come round and spend a few nights with me at the Holiday Inn at the airport. And — and I *want him* to. I want to live with him *permanently* at the Holiday Inn at the airport because I *fancy him legless*. And. Because I've never had *a Scotsman*.

PATRICK: I — Oh Sandra!

SANDRA: And your book tells me Ronnie blocks everything that's best in me.

PATRICK: San-dra!

SANDRA: But your book *doesn't* tell me what to do about the boring bloody stupid spoilt brats Ronnie had by me. Or what to do every time I think about them sitting round his stupid-looking red plastic breakfast table.

PATRICK: I —

SANDRA: Sitting round it, I said, *eating their breakfast without me.* (What?)

PATRICK: My book, Sandra.

SANDRA: I could give you your book back, I suppose.

PATRICK: Never mind your Scotsman! (What?)

SANDRA: I could give it back, but do you think your book could tell me that I can leave Ronnie's children behind me and never think about them at the breakfast table *again*?

PATRICK: Well you haven't read the whole book, Sandra.

SANDRA: If I did read it, could it tell me what I want to hear?

PATRICK: I —

SANDRA: Could it?

[*Enter* RENA *with a lamp.*]

RENA: Patrick Nauldie!

[PATRICK *puts the box of condoms away.* RENA *goes to set up the lamp.* SANDRA *goes to the gramophone.*]

I hope you've calmed down, now, Patrick Nauldie.

PATRICK: I —

RENA: Sandra!

[RENA *and* SANDRA *stop work simultaneously.*]

Where have you been?

SANDRA: I —

RENA: Patrick Nauldie insulted me because of you. So please return his book to him: he's been *desperate*.

SANDRA: OK.

[*She efficiently produces* PATRICK's *manuscript in silent triumph.*]

PATRICK: Oh no.

[SANDRA *gives it to* RENA.]

SANDRA: Read it, Mother.

RENA: Oh ah —

SANDRA: Read it. There's not much time.

PATRICK: I — Yes, read it, Mother.

SANDRA: It's a masterpiece.

PATRICK: Read it. I — You only read four and half pages, Sandra, you can't say it's a —

SANDRA: It's a masterpiece!

PATRICK: I — You're right. Just read it, Mother.

[RENA *looks bewilderedly between the manuscript and her children.*]

SANDRA: [*Helpfully*] Just choose a few bits to read, Mother.

PATRICK: No.

SANDRA: Yes. There isn't —

PATRICK: You've got to read it all.

SANDRA: There isn't —

PATRICK: To get the wider argument.

SANDRA: There probably isn't time for her to get the wider argument. Is there, Mum?

PATRICK: I –

SANDRA: And anyway: I didn't need the wider argument. So read, Mother.

PATRICK: I – You needed the wider argument *more than anyone*.

SANDRA: Read.

RENA: 'Chapter Four. Bridget the Slave.' Who –? Who's Bridget the Slave? Oh ha-ha. That must be me. Now: 'My mother was made pathetic and passive by her husband and family.' Aye, Patrick. So I was, son. But I've changed for the better since then. Because just think: if the big bomb dropped tomorrow, it wouldn't make the slightest bit of difference to me. Ha-ha.

SANDRA: Read, Mother.

PATRICK: You misread my book.

PATRICK: Separating doesn't mean a Scotsman and a few nights at the Holiday Inn.

SANDRA: What more do you want?

PATRICK: You misread my book.

SANDRA: I'll read your book how I want to read it. And you –

PATRICK: I –

RENA: Patrick Nauldie: when you were seventeen and dragged me into that Job Centre, saying, 'Give me something to *respect*, Mother', you weren't half as humiliated as me. No. Because when that obnoxious wee clerical type said to me, 'Have you got any cleaning *experience*, Mrs Nauldie' in a loud voice, I took *palpitations*.

PATRICK: I –

RENA: And you had the *cheek* to say, 'Take it, Mother, it's a start.'

PATRICK: You walked out and left me standing there.

RENA: 'It's a start.' I'll – I know I did. So it's just as well I've got this sense of humour of mine, isn't –?

SANDRA: Just read, Mother.

RENA: Isn't it? Yes, just as well I'm the practical type now-adays. Oh yes, Sandra.

SANDRA: Mother!

RENA: Because as long as people buy your wee book, Patrick, you can insult me to your heart's content.

SANDRA: I –

RENA: *All right*, Sandra. You're –

SANDRA: Read!

RENA: You're not dominating me.

SANDRA: I –

[*She starts laughing.*]

RENA: You proud of me, son? Because did you hear me? I said to her, 'You're not dominating *me*.' Now [*flicking through the manuscript*]: 'Chapter Six. Constable Nauldie. The . . . Small . . . Time . . . Tyrant. The Small –' [*Roars with laughter.*] Willie? Look at this, Willie. Come on.

[*She picks up the patch of carpet, rolls it a little and starts beating the prostrate* WILLIE *with it.*]

WILLIE: Bridget! Heh –

SANDRA: Look, Patrick –

WILLIE: Bridget.

SANDRA: Your book's working.

PATRICK: I –

RENA: You've been a pig for thirty years, Willie Nauldie.

[WILLIE *suddenly sits up sharply.* RENA *starts jabbing* WILLIE'*s face with the manuscript.*]

RENA: So read it. It'll change your life. It'll *kill* you.

WILLIE: I – OK, woman. [*Suddenly focuses as* RENA *stops.*] 'My father's ways of maintaining power included keeping me so short of pocket-money that when I wanted to save up for my own set of bagpipes, I had to steal fifty pence from his jacket pocket every week until I –'

RENA: Patrick Nauldie: you're *still* writing a load of shite.

WILLIE: I – 'And they never knew about it.' Aye, that's where you're wrong, boy.

PATRICK: I – You *didn't* know about it.

WILLIE: We –

PATRICK: Because you would have done something if you'd known about it.

WILLIE: We *did* do something.

RENA: How could we *not* know, Patrick?

WILLIE: We didn't *increase* your pocket-money. Ha-ha.

RENA: We were *poor* people.

[*Pause.* WILLIE *finishes getting up.*]

PATRICK: Is this true?

WILLIE: What did you want me to do?

PATRICK: I –

WILLIE: Arrest you?

PATRICK: Because I can't –

WILLIE: Heh Sergeant McIntyre, sir, I want to charge my eleven-year-old son with –

PATRICK: I can't –

RENA: So we just laughed, didn't we?

WILLIE: With stealing fifty pence off me. Ha-ha.

PATRICK: I can't publish *lies.*

[*He goes to the phone and starts dialling.* WILLIE *starts to flick through the manuscript.*]

So that means I'll have to get the book *changed.*

RENA: *I* don't mind a few lies.

SANDRA: Lies or no lies: your book works, Patrick. Leave it alone.

PATRICK: I – I'll have to. Ah –

[*It is clear that* PATRICK *cannot remember the whole number. He puts down the receiver.*]

Where did you put my correspondence, Mother?

WILLIE: Chapter Ten.

RENA: I –

WILLIE: 'Patrick Nauldie.'

[SANDRA *discovers the folder where* PATRICK *left it and goes to pick it up.*]

'Jailbird and Criminal.' I – Right, Bridget.

[SANDRA *hands the folder to* PATRICK.]

Out the room.

RENA: Och Willie: that bit's just a joke. Isn't it, Sandra?

WILLIE: Bridget.

SANDRA: No, Mum.

[PATRICK *takes out an envelope and gives the folder back to* SANDRA.]

WILLIE: Out the room.

RENA: Patrick just made that bit up, Willie, for the story. Didn't you, Patrick?

[PATRICK *starts dialling, referring to the letter.*]

PATRICK: No, Mum.

WILLIE: Bridget.

RENA: Well your father would have heard if you were a criminal, Patrick.

SANDRA: But it's all right, Mum.

RENA: Because your father's a highly respected police officer. Aren't you, Willie?

WILLIE: You can't hear this, Bridget.

SANDRA: It's all right, Dad.

RENA: I can hear this.

WILLIE: You're the refined type.

SANDRA: Because Patrick's reformed now. Look at his clothes.

[PATRICK *finishes dialling.*]

RENA: Well, don't you worry, Patrick. Even if you're a rapist or a murderer, I'll still stand by you.

WILLIE: I –

[*Pause.* SANDRA *diverts to looking through the folder.* WILLIE *returns to the manuscript.*]

WILLIE: 'So I waited till I was twenty-one before I became a criminal. I waited till I knew I could request for my parents not to be informed. In retrospect this seems a cowardly –'

RENA: Ha-ha. Yes, my Patrick always was the writing type.

WILLIE: 'I should have become a criminal *from the start* and isolated myself *openly*. And in conclusion I have begun to find my prison career so satisfying that I will be sorry to see it discontinued.' I see. Now –

[*He puts down the manuscript.*]

RENA: I mean: even as a child he used to sit up at his father's bureau and write a load of shite.

PATRICK: [*Into the receiver*] Can I speak to Mr Bedford, please?

SANDRA: You've got a lot of letters, Patrick.

PATRICK: Mr Bedford, please, [*To* SANDRA] (What, Sandra?)

SANDRA: In fact, Patrick: you got a lot of *rejections*.

PATRICK: I –

SANDRA: [*Flicking idly through the folder*] 'We are sorry, but –' 'We are sorry but –'

PATRICK: I –

SANDRA: 'We are sorry –'

PATRICK: All right, Sandra! (Sorry.) [*Into the receiver*] Mr Bedford.

[SANDRA *puts down the folder.*]

[*To* SANDRA] I save them up, to prove people *wrong*. Ha.

SANDRA: Ha.

[*She refers to* PATRICK's *manuscript.*]

RENA: Oh yes. I used to say to him, 'What are you writing, Patrick?' He'd go, 'I'm writing my reports, woman. Away and play.' Ha-ha. Seven years old. So nothing's changed, has it? 'Away and play.' Ha-ha.

SANDRA: [*Has traced where* WILLIE *was reading and echoes:*] 'Sorry to see it discontinued.'

PATRICK: Can you ask him to ring me as soon as he comes back, please? It's urgent. This is Patrick Nauldie on —

PATRICK: [*Underneath* SANDRA] On 0597 57643. Thank you.

SANDRA: Patrick. Tell me something, Patrick.

[*He puts down the receiver.*]

PATRICK: What, Sandra?

SANDRA: Why doesn't it say anything about you being released?

PATRICK: I —

WILLIE: Oh don't ask him.

PATRICK: I —

WILLIE: Just don't ask him.

PATRICK: Because, everybody, I haven't been released. Ta-ra!

WILLIE: I —

[PATRICK *starts to undress and reveals prison clothes underneath.*]

PATRICK: Because after I walked out of prison, everybody, I stole this, and this, and these, and this to please you, to *impress* you, to make you listen. I realize now that I should also have presented my *criminality* to you, openly. Because no matter what I do, no matter what I say, no matter what I *write*, you're not *ever* going to listen. Ha-ha.

SANDRA: I listened to you, Patrick. But, as per usual, I don't count.

PATRICK: They'll be coming to pick me up maybe any minute now, if I let them, and, quite frankly, I wouldn't mind being back for tomorrow's breakfast.

SANDRA: I —

PATRICK: (You know?)

WILLIE: Patrick Nauldie, you —

RENA: Willie.

WILLIE: You —

RENA: You can't arrest Patrick. He's going to keep us, in future.

WILLIE: Bridget.

[*Pause.*]

So, Patrick Nauldie: you're under arrest.

[*He goes to pick up the receiver.* PATRICK *stops him.*]

PATRICK: By you and whose police force?

WILLIE: I –

PATRICK: You're not arresting me, Dad –

WILLIE: You –

PATRICK: I'm giving myself up.

[*The phone rings.* PATRICK *picks up the receiver.*]

RENA: And anyway, Willie –

PATRICK: Mr Bedford?

RENA: You can't arrest Patrick.

PATRICK: Patrick Nauldie here, Mr Bedford.

RENA: You've handed in your notice.

WILLIE: I –

SANDRA: Leave your book, Patrick.

WILLIE: What are you talking about, woman?

SANDRA: Just leave it exactly as it –

PATRICK: I just wanted to give you some last minute cha–... You wrote to me at the prison –? ... Ah, oh – *What?* But it says here that 'Family Atrocities' is a particularly fine example of the prison-writing genre which is very much in fashion at the moment. And that provided all concerned could come to an agreement you would very much like to pub–... Your lawyers?

SANDRA: Oh, ah –

PATRICK: They –?

SANDRA: Tell him we wouldn't dream of suing, Patrick.

PATRICK: You're *sorry*?

RENA: Oh don't worry, son.

WILLIE: Right, Bridget, that's it.

[PATRICK *holds the receiver away from himself. The voice continues.*]

RENA: Don't worry.

WILLIE: No more luxuries. Ha-ha.

[SANDRA *takes the receiver from* PATRICK.]

SANDRA: Is that Mr Bedford? Mr Bedford: I'm Patrick Nauldie's big sister, and you can take it from me that none of us here will take any –

WILLIE: In fact, Bridget –

PATRICK: Give up, Sandra.

SANDRA: The prison authorities might –? [*To* PATRICK] (No, Patrick.) [*Into the receiver*] I – Surely the prison authorities would –

PATRICK: Just give up.

WILLIE: If –

[SANDRA *puts down the receiver.*]

RENA: Because, Patrick, son, even if I'm living in a vagrant's hostel by then, I'll still provide you with a roof over your head and a bed for the night.

[*Pause.*]

WILLIE: Because if I've –

SANDRA: I – (What, Dad?)

WILLIE: If I've resigned, Bridget, there'll be no more. *Nothing.* Ha-ha.

SANDRA: I –

WILLIE: Because who'd employ me? (What?)

SANDRA: Dad: you haven't handed in your notice. Because I told your colleague to cover up for you.

WILLIE: I –

SANDRA: And, as a matter of fact, he said he was used to covering up for you.

RENA: Aye, I've spent my life covering up for Willie Nauldie. Everyone else might as well join in.

[*Pause.*]

SANDRA: But why, Patrick?

PATRICK: I —

SANDRA: Why give up?

PATRICK: It's not worth it.

SANDRA: I — I mean: you came here for a confrontation, didn't you?

PATRICK: I —

SANDRA: So what I want to know is: where the hell is it?

PATRICK: A confrontation, Sandra?

SANDRA: Yes, you came home to behave like a criminal.

PATRICK: I didn't really want a confrontation, Sandra.

SANDRA: So why don't you *start*? (What?)

PATRICK: I thought *you* wanted one.

SANDRA: I —

PATRICK: I thought you all wanted one and I came home to give you what I thought you wanted. And when I came home, when I arrived home at first, I thought that I was right. Because otherwise why didn't you all walk out the door instead of inventing pathetic excuses to stay?

SANDRA: I — What's this about, Patrick?

PATRICK: And I *was* right, *Sandra*. You *did* all want a confrontation. But not to make things better: oh no. You all wanted a confrontation to make things worse.

SANDRA: It doesn't matter if your book isn't perfect.

PATRICK: I —

SANDRA: Who cares if there's a few errors in —?

PATRICK: A few?

SANDRA: I know I don't.

PATRICK: Because let's face it, Sandra: my book's *all* errors.

SANDRA: I —

PATRICK: My book's a load of shite. (You were right, Mother.) Ha-ha.

RENA: Ha-ha.

SANDRA: I —

PATRICK: Take the last chapter of my book, everybody. It's called 'My Plan for the Family'.

RENA: I –

PATRICK: Basically that plan involved one thing and one thing only –

RENA: Oh Patrick: you can't plan for families. Ha-ha.

PATRICK: Ha-ha. I know, Mother. So one thing and one thing only: doing away with the family. All families. So I came home to tell you that's what you all wanted. But it's not what you want. No. I came home to tell you that you all wanted to be set free. But you don't. I came home to tell you that you all wanted to stop destroying each other. But you don't. I came home to tell you that you're all irrelevant to each other. But –

RENA: Patrick Nauldie –

PATRICK: But you don't care. I – In fact –

RENA: Is that one of your insults?

PATRICK: You *enjoy* being irrelevant to each other.

RENA: Because quite frankly, Patrick Nauldie, I don't understand it.

PATRICK: I –

SANDRA: It means we're all out for what we can get, Mother.

PATRICK: It means we *think* we are all out for what we can get and we *think* we want to change, but actually we want to stay *exactly as we are* and *fantasize* about what we can get.

SANDRA: Well I'm changing, because –

RENA: I –

SANDRA: Because *I'm* out to get what *I* want in future.

RENA: You are not changing, Sandra.

PATRICK: I –

RENA: And neither are you, Patrick Nauldie. Because you two have always been taking what you can get from me –

WILLIE: I –

RENA: Always: even if I had to starve. (What?)

WILLIE: Patrick Nauldie: you're under arrest.

[WILLIE *goes to the phone and picks up the receiver.*]

PATRICK: I told you, Dad.

[WILLIE *starts to dial.*]

You're not arresting me.

WILLIE: Is Sergeant McIntyre there, please –?

[PATRICK *hits* WILLIE *clean away from the phone.* WILLIE *topples and falls.*]

PATRICK: I'm giving myself up.

RENA: Yes, maybe you should, Patrick.

PATRICK: I –

[RENA *starts tidying up* PATRICK's *clothes.*]

Prison's the best place for you: you're a criminal.

SANDRA: Well your book worked for me, Patrick.

[PATRICK *produces the knife from the bag.*]

RENA: Ah, Patrick, you –

[PATRICK *seems to advance towards* SANDRA. RENA *stands in front of* SANDRA.]

You'll have to kill your old mother first, Patrick Nauldie. You *criminal.*

[*He swerves nonchalantly to the telephone and cuts the wire.*]

PATRICK: Sorry, Mother, I – For what it's worth, I assure you that none of this is giving me any pleasure. I'm merely making sure that my father isn't going to arrest me.

SANDRA: Patrick –

PATRICK: Or dominate me.

SANDRA: Will you understand that you are a success?

PATRICK: I –

SANDRA: Look at what you've achieved: I'm separating.

PATRICK: You're separating for entirely the wrong reasons, Sandra. [*Produces the box of condoms from the discarded clothes.*] Because you –

SANDRA: No, Patrick, don't –

PATRICK: Present from Scotland, Sandra?

SANDRA: You prude.

PATRICK: I —
SANDRA: You're a prude and you *don't like people.*

[*Pause.*]

PATRICK: Maybe I don't, Sandra.
SANDRA: I —
PATRICK: But at least I'm not a liar.
SANDRA: I —
PATRICK: Because present from Scotland, Sandra? For Ronnie?
SANDRA: You —
PATRICK: At three dollars fifty a packet?

[*He goes to throw the box at her.*]

SANDRA: What's so good about telling the truth?
PATRICK: I —

[*He drops the box at his feet. Pause.*]

RENA: Could I perhaps have one of your wee johnnies, Sandra? I'll go out and get a man for the night.

[*Pause. He puts the knife down.*]

PATRICK: So, see your . . . johnnies, Sandra.
SANDRA: You —
PATRICK: Your American johnnies, they — In fact, see your bagpipes — your American bagpipes — they make me sick.

[*He picks up the bagpipes.*]

SANDRA: They make *me* sick.
PATRICK: I —

[SANDRA *picks up the knife.*]

SANDRA: Americans make me sick.

[*She takes hold of the other end of the bagpipes and starts shredding them.*]

PATRICK: You're talking shite, Sandra.
SANDRA: Americans make me really sick.

PATRICK: You came home to Scotland to take my mother home with you.

SANDRA: I —

PATRICK: To impress these Americans.

SANDRA: I wanted to take my mother home so I could have a right good *confrontation* now and again. Just like this one.

RENA: Well, Patrick Nauldie —

SANDRA: And — What's wrong with that?

RENA: I wouldn't mind if —

SANDRA: So I'll take my mother anywhere I choose and you won't stop me.

[*They drop the shredded bagpipes.*]

RENA: I wouldn't mind impressing a few Americans.

[*Pause.* PATRICK *starts laughing and scatters the bagpipes across the carpet with his feet.* WILLIE *is, by now, rousing and rising.*]

I — His carpet, Patrick.

WILLIE: My carpet, Patrick.

[*He turns to* PATRICK *and hits him.*]

RENA: His carpet.

WILLIE: My carpet.

[*He again hits* PATRICK.]

RENA: His carpet.

WILLIE: My carpet.

[*He again hits* PATRICK, *who falls.* SANDRA *goes to tend* PATRICK. RENA *diverts to* PATRICK's *suit and starts folding it.*]

RENA: So I might just come to America with you, Sandra.

SANDRA: Oh no you're not, Mother.

RENA: I —

SANDRA: I'm coming back to Scotland.

RENA: At least for a holiday.

SANDRA: I'm not ever going back to America.

RENA: Because it's awful violent in Scotland.

[*Pause.*]

And because I've never even met my grandchildren.

[*She finds the money in the suit.* WILLIE *finds the cut phone wire.* SANDRA *undoes* PATRICK's *boots.*]

WILLIE: Well, at one point, if I'd've found my phone out of order, I'd've — I'd've — I'd've *hit* someone. Ha-ha. Where's my whisky?

RENA: Ha-ha. So you'll have to save up your overtime and send me to America, Willie. We'll need every penny we can get our hands on. [*Pockets the money.*] Because I'll have to show my grandchildren that not all women are like their mother. No, not all women are out for what they can get.

[*She puts the folded suit with the luggage.*]

WILLIE: Aye, you've been awful unlucky with your family, Bridget. My whisky, I says.

[*Having taken one of* PATRICK's *boots off,* SANDRA *opens the bureau to reveal the whisky and returns to remove* PATRICK's *other boot, while* WILLIE *goes to pick up the bottle and takes it with glasses to the table.*]

I'll miss them all the same. When they go.

RENA: Oh no. I've definitely got my blessings to count. My grandchildren are getting the outdoor life with — with Ronnie. My children are getting what they want. And my husband's going to his grave a bad drunken pig with my blood on his police uniform. Ha-ha.

WILLIE: Ha-ha.

[SANDRA *finds the special message as she removes* PATRICK's *other boot.*]

SANDRA: Who did you send this *to*, Mother?

RENA: I — [*Looks at it.*] Patrick Nauldie: you disobedient swine. I trusted you to deliver my special message.

SANDRA: [*Reading*] Dear Miss —

RENA: No, Sandra —

SANDRA: 'I found your letter to my Willie.'

RENA: Sandra. Don't. Ha-ha.

SANDRA: 'And I thought you might like to know that my Willie puts his willie into many different women. And I know for a fact that my Willie never washes his willie afterwards. That's why I, personally, never let my Willie put his willie into *me*. This is being delivered to you by my nine-year-old son. Just thank him. No reply necessary. P.S. I always try to see the funny side of things.'

[WILLIE *goes to the records.* RENA *returns to the suit.*]

RENA: Ha-ha. Imagine me. Being jealous of him.

WILLIE: Jim Reeves?

RENA: Him?

WILLIE: The man's a genius. No doubt about it.

RENA: And totally unlovable.

WILLIE: The matter is not —

RENA: Yes, but you've your work to go to.

WILLIE: The subject is closed.

[WILLIE *selects a record and puts it on, but does not switch on yet.* PATRICK *gets up and starts putting his shoes on.* SANDRA *hands him his manuscript.*]

SANDRA: We'll send your book to America, Patrick.

PATRICK: I —

SANDRA: They'll publish it in America.

PATRICK: You don't like America.

SANDRA: I — Patrick: we'll use America.

[PATRICK *throws the manuscript in the air, and it falls to the floor.* WILLIE *pours two whiskies. Horn is tooted.* RENA *fixes the lamp she brought in earlier.*]

SANDRA: I —

WILLIE: These young cops.

RENA: Right, Willie.

WILLIE: Bridget.
RENA: To your work.

> [WILLIE *hands* RENA *the tartan skirt. He changes into the tartan jacket. Horn is tooted.* SANDRA *starts collecting the luggage and manuscript.*]

SANDRA: Lift anywhere, Patrick?
PATRICK: I – Who's driving, Sandra?
SANDRA: My Scotsman, Patrick . . . Is that a problem?
PATRICK: I – No, Sandra. We'll *use* your Scotsman.
SANDRA: I. Exactly . . . You coming, Mum?

> [RENA *finishes putting on her skirt, picks up the suit and hands it to* PATRICK.]

RENA: I – [*Turns swiftly away from her children.*] There'd've been no point in me getting a house, Willie.
WILLIE: Bridget.

> [*He hands* RENA *a glass of whisky.*]

RENA: You'd only have been round every other day for soup.
WILLIE: I – Och I'd've bought in a couple of slaves. Ha-ha.
RENA: Ha-ha.

> [*Horn is tooted.* PATRICK *finishes with his shoes.*]

SANDRA: Patrick?
PATRICK: I – To the police station?
SANDRA: Yes, Patrick. To the police station.
PATRICK: Whatever.

> [*Exit.*]

SANDRA: I –

> [WILLIE *switches on the record.* SANDRA, *having picked up her cases, is very heavily laden; she moves to go. 'You're the Only Good Thing That's Happened to Me' comes on.* WILLIE *takes the drink out of* RENA's *hand and puts it down. Exit* SANDRA *as* WILLIE *takes* RENA *in a wondrously skilful dance and lights fade.*]

Waiting for Shuggie's Ma

Characters

GUS
STU
} Two sixteen-year-old boys

Setting

A veranda on the top floor of a block of flats in Glasgow.
There is a clothes-line with sheets, which are all but concealing the glass door and windows at the back of the veranda.

Waiting for Shuggie's Ma was given a rehearsed reading at the Royal Exchange Theatre, Manchester, on 14 September 1986 with the following cast:

GUS	*Iain Heggie*
STU	*Robert Clare*

Director: Michael Fox

GUS *and* STU *are found on, standing at the front of the veranda.*

GUS: It's good up here but.
STU: Aye. (No bad.)
GUS: It's brilliant.
STU: *Oh* aye. (Aye.)

   [*Pause.*]

GUS: Thirty-five floors and all.
STU: Aye. (No.)
GUS: Thirty-five floors to the top of the building. (What?)
STU: Is it fuck.
GUS: What?
STU: Is it fuck thirty-five floors to the top of the building.
GUS: No?
STU: No!
GUS: Aw.

   [*Pause.*]

STU: Thirty-*four* floors.
GUS: Eh?
STU: Thirty-*four* floors to the top of the building.
GUS: Aye?
STU: Aye!
GUS: Aw.

   [*Pause.*]

   At least you see dead far.
STU: Aye.
GUS: At least you see dead far from the top of the building.
STU: You see right across Glasgow from the top of the building.
GUS: You see to Manchester from the top of the building.
STU: You see to – Can you fuck.
GUS: You see to – (What?)
STU: Can you fuck see to Manchester from the top of the building.

GUS: No?

STU: No.

GUS: Aw.

[*Pause.*]

Well we can see the Boys' Brigade from the top of the building.

STU: Aye.

GUS: The Boys' Brigade Hall.

STU: Aye. (Definitely, man.)

GUS: Aye?

STU: Aye!

GUS: Aw.

[*Pause.*]

And the Boys' Brigade get out in a minute.

STU: Aye. (*Oh* aye.)

GUS: Aye. Out for their wee break.

STU: Aye. Out for their fly smoke.

GUS: Aye. Out for a scratch of their balls.

STU: Aye. Out for a sly slash up against a wall.

GUS: Aye. Out for a quick wank.

STU: Aye. (No!)

GUS: (Ha-ha.)

STU: *Oh* no. Quick wank nothing!

GUS: Aye, quick wank ha-ha but!

STU: Quick wank ha-ha?

GUS: Aye, because –

STU: Oh *aye.* Ha-ha *definitely.*

GUS: Because the Boys' Brigade are a *right* toss-off squad.

STU: Aye.

GUS: Aye?

STU: Aye!

GUS: Aw.

[*Pause.*]

GUS: So the Boys' Brigade wanks are due out.

STU: Aye.

GUS: And. The Boys' Brigade wanks will look about.

STU: *Oh* aye. (Definitely.)

GUS: Look up and see *us*.

STU: No.

GUS: Look up and see *me*.

STU: No!

GUS: And I'll flash my arse.

STU: No. (*Oh* no.)

GUS: No?

STU: No!

GUS: Aw.

[*Pause.*]

STU: Because when the Boys' Brigade wanks look up, they won't see you.

GUS: Aw.

STU: They won't see me.

GUS: Aw.

STU: They'll see two dots at the top of the building.

GUS: Aw.

[*Pause.*]

Two dots at the top of the building?

STU: Aye.

GUS: Aw.

[*Pause.*]

It is good up here but, *isn't it*?

STU: Aye. (No bad.)

GUS: I mean: see Shuggie's ma's sheets, right?

STU: These sheets here?

GUS: Aye. These sheets here. Brilliant, aren't they?

STU: No.

GUS: Brilliant sheets! (What?)

STU: No.

GUS: No?

STU: No!
GUS: Aw.

[*Pause.*]

STU: Wank sheets.
GUS: Aw.
STU: Bastard sheets.
GUS: Aw.
STU: Fucking Boys' Brigade headbanger sheets.
GUS: Aw.

[*Pause.*]

It's good up here but.
STU: Aye. (No bad.)
GUS: It's good up here waiting for Shuggie's ma.
STU: Aye, *no*! (Is it fuck.)
GUS: No?
STU: No!
GUS: Aw.
STU: It's bastarding boring waiting for Shuggie's ma.
GUS: Aw.
STU: So Shuggie's ma bastarding better hurry up.
GUS: Aw.

[*Pause.*]

At least the top of the building shakes.
STU: Aye.
GUS: Shakes in the wind.
STU: *Oh* aye. It shakes like a zombie.
GUS: Aye. It shakes like a bastard.
STU: Aye. It shakes like a dick.
GUS: Aye. It shakes like a bastarding zombie.
STU: Aye. It shakes like a bastarding zombie's dick.
GUS: Aye. It shakes like –

[*Pause.*]

Like a bastarding zombie's dick?

STU: Aye.
GUS: Aw.

  [*Pause.*]

  And Shuggie's ma's hoose is brilliant.
STU: Aye, *no!* And is it fuck.
GUS: Is it fuck?
STU: Aye, is it fuck.
GUS: Aw.
STU: It's a pure dive.
GUS: Aw.

  [*Pause.*]

STU: So who gived you the keys?
GUS: Eh? (So I met Shuggie.)
STU: Who gived you the keys to Shuggie's ma's hoose?
GUS: I met Shuggie and he gave me the keys to his ma's
  hoose. Aye, I met the cunt, I got him to come across with
  the keys. I met the bastard, the bastard's on his way to the
  Boys' Brigade. I met him, I threatened to bop the bampot
  one on the nut, he doesn't come across with the keys to his
  ma's hoose. He says, 'I'll give you the keys to my ma's
  hoose if you promise not to mark my ma's good furniture.'
  So I says, 'I'll mark you, you don't come across with the
  keys. You don't walk across with the keys, Shuggie boy, I'll
  walk across you.'
STU: Aye, and you know *what*, Gus?
GUS: *What*, Stu?
STU: You mark Shuggie's ma's good furniture, *Shuggie's ma*
  will mark you.
GUS: Shuggie's ma?
STU: Aye, Shuggie's ma.
GUS: Aw.

  [*Pause.*]

STU: Because Shuggie's ma is a big bird.
GUS: Aw.

[*Pause.*]

So how will we know when Shuggie's ma's back?

STU: What?

GUS: We're out on Shuggie's ma's veranda, so how will we know when Shuggie's ma's back in her hoose?

STU: We'll see her.

GUS: How will we know she's back from the bingo?

STU: We'll see Shuggie's ma coming in at the bottom of the building.

GUS: Aw.

[*Pause.*]

No! We will *not* see Shuggie's ma at the bottom of the building.

STU: How come?

GUS: Because Shuggie's ma will be a dot at the bottom of the building.

STU: So?

GUS: So we won't know which dot at the bottom of the building Shuggie's ma *is*.

STU: Aye.

GUS: No.

STU: Aye, we *will*.

GUS: How come?

STU: Because Shuggie's ma will be a red dot at the bottom of the building.

GUS: Aw.

STU: Because Shuggie's ma wears a red coat.

GUS: Aw.

[*They look down. Pause.*]

STU: The only trouble is, Gus –

GUS: What's that, Stu?

STU: It's also bastarding boring looking down at the bottom of the building.

GUS: Bastarding boring?

STU: Aye.

GUS: Aw.

  [*Pause.*]

  So, Stu.

STU: What, Gus?

GUS: Do you remember I gave a Boys' Brigade wank a
  tanking?

STU: The time you . . . you . . .

GUS: A tanking outside the Boys' Brigade Hall.

STU: Aye? Aye, *oh* aye. (*Definitely* some tanking you gave the
  wank.)

GUS: So he says to me, he says, 'So, cunt, you are the only
  cunt *here* is not in the Boys' Brigade, cunt.'

STU: Aye. Oh aye, Gus. Because then you says, you says, 'Too
  fucking right, cunt. And that's why you've had it. Aye,
  you, cunt, are going to get bopped.'

GUS: I did.

STU: Brilliant, man.

GUS: Was I?

STU: Aye.

GUS: Was I brilliant?

STU: *Oh* aye.

GUS: Aw.

  [*Pause.*]

  So ho. So: the wank swung a couple of miss-hit bops at
  us. (Soft cunt.)

STU: So you kneed him one to the balls.

GUS: Aye. I bopped him one to the belly.

STU: Aye. You butted him one on the nut.

GUS: Aye. And I pinned him on the ground.

STU: Aye. And you –

GUS: And I –

STU: And you –

GUS: And I practically farted in his fucking face. Ha-ha. Aye.
  (The cunt.)

[*Pause.*]

So it was a *clear fucking victory*.

STU: *Oh* aye.

GUS: But did you hear what the cheeky cunt says to us but?

STU: (Definitely.)

GUS: He says, 'Do you give in?'

STU: Aye.

GUS: 'Do you give in?'

STU: *Oh* aye.

GUS: The mental fucking headbanger Boys' Brigade wank
merchant . . . And it was a clear fucking victory too. A clear
fucking victory, so he shoots up the road to fuck, bleeding
to bastardy. (The cunt.)

STU: Aye.

GUS: Aye, and he shoots up the road *right into* Shuggie's ma.

STU: Aye. Right into Shuggie's ma.

GUS: Shuggie's fucking ma.

STU: Shuggie's ma who takes the cunt –

GUS: Fucking *takes* the cunt.

STU: The cunt who – (This bit's brilliant.)

GUS: This is the best bit.

STU: The Boys' Brigade wank merchant!

GUS: So she takes the Boys' Brigade wank merchant up to her
hoose here.

STU: Aye.

GUS: Up to her hoose here and the Boys' Brigade wank
merchant does not get to emerge, does not get to get *out*, for
a full *two hours* later.

STU: *Oh* no.

GUS: No.

STU: That *was* the best bit.

GUS: That bit *was* brilliant.

STU: *Oh* aye.

GUS: Aye. Aye?

STU: Aye.

GUS: Aw.

GUS: There's the –

STU: Where?

GUS: There's the Boys' Brigade out for their wee break. (Eh?)

STU: Out for their fly smoke.

GUS: All the black dots outside the Boys' Brigade Hall.

STU: *Oh* aye.

GUS: Aye. (Out for their sly slash.)

STU: Aye, well –

GUS: Aye. Out for their quick wank.

STU: Aye, well –

GUS: Quick wank ha-ha but!

STU: Aye, well, just keep looking for Shuggie's ma. (Ha-ha fuck off.)

GUS: Ha-ha fuck off?

STU: Ha-ha fuck off!

GUS: Aw.

[*Long pause.*]

So, Stu.

STU: What, Gus?

GUS: Let's *show* these Boys' Brigade wanks.

STU: No, we –

GUS: Because –

STU: No –

GUS: Because –

STU: They'll look up and see a couple of dots at the top of the building.

GUS: *Eh?*

STU: Two dots in front of Shuggie's ma's sheets.

GUS: Shuggie's ma's sheets?

STU: Aye.

GUS: Shuggie's ma's *sheets*?

STU: *Oh* aye.

GUS: Aw.

[*Pause. He yanks a sheet off the line and starts waving it over the veranda.*]

STU: What is this?
GUS: Haw you Boys' Brigade wanks.
STU: What *the fuck* is this?
GUS: You Boys' Brigade tools.

[STU *takes the other sheet off the line.*]

You cunts. You wanks. Look at me.

[STU *starts waving.*]

STU: Look at *us*.
GUS: Aye, look at us.
STU: You tools.
GUS: You headbangers.
STU: You *Boys' Brigade* headbangers.
GUS: }
STU: } Fuck bastarding off.

[*Pause. They stop waving.*]

GUS: Think the Boys' Brigade wanks saw us waving at them, Stu?
STU: I don't know, Gus . . . Because they are nothing but a bunch of black dots outside the Boys' Brigade Hall.
GUS: Aw.

[*Pause.*]

Heh Stu.
STU: What, Gus?
GUS: But what if they see the two dots *climbing down* Shuggie's ma's sheets?
STU: Eh?
GUS: Climbing down Shuggie's ma's veranda to the veranda below?
STU: No.
GUS: No?
STU: *Oh* no.
GUS: Aw.

[*Pause.*]

STU: Because: they'll look up and see –
GUS: They'll look up and see –
STU: They'll see –

GUS: ⎫
STU: ⎭   *Two dots* climbing down Shuggie's ma's sheets.

[*Pause.*]

STU: So they won't know who –
GUS: Heh Stu.
STU: They won't know who the two dots are. (What, Gus?)
GUS: They will know who the two dots are, because Shuggie'll tell them.

[*Pause.*]

STU: I'm not climbing down no building.
GUS: No?
STU: No. (I'm meeting Shuggie's ma.)
GUS: Aw.
STU: And if I *did* climb down the building, I'd be fucked if I'd climb back up it.
GUS: Aw.

[*Pause.*]

STU: Besides, the black dots have fucked off.
GUS: Fucked off?
STU: Aye.
GUS: Oh *no*.
STU: Aye. Fucked off from outside the Boys' Brigade Hall.
GUS: Aw.

[*Pause.*]

The Boys' Brigade must've gone back in.
STU: Aye.
GUS: After their 'wee break'.

STU: *Oh* aye.

GUS: So do you think the Boys' Brigade wanks saw us, Stu? (Surely to fuck.)

STU: I don't know.

GUS: They must've seen us waving Shuggie's ma's sheets(?)

STU: I don't know.

GUS: Because –

STU: Ssshhh . . . (I heard a cunt.)

[*Pause.*]

GUS: What cunt was that?

STU: Sssh . . . I'm sure I heard a cunt *walking about.*

[*Pause.*]

GUS: Heh. Cunt. Who the fuck are you?

STU: Sssshhh . . . (It must be Shuggie's ma.)

GUS: Shuggie's *ma*?

STU: Aye.

GUS: Aw.

[*Pause.*]

Oh no.

STU: Oh *yes. Definitely* Shuggie's ma.

[GUS *looks about.*]

GUS: Heh Stu.

STU: Heh Gus.

GUS: We forgot to keep on looking down.

STU: I wonder what Shuggie's ma will do to me.

GUS: *I* forgot to keep on looking down.

STU: What Shuggie's ma will do *to my body*.

GUS: Down at the bottom of the building.

STU: Or what she'll make *me* do to *her* body.

GUS: Because it was bastarding boring looking down. (Stu.)

[*Pause.*]

Sorry.

STU: It's all right.

GUS: Is it all right?

STU: Aye.

GUS: Aw.

[*Pause.*]

GUS: And heh Stu.

STU: What, Gus?

GUS: What's all those black dots at the bottom of the building . . . ? Those black dots *coming in* the building?

[*They look down together and at each other.*]

GUS:⎫
STU:⎭ It's the Boys' Brigade!

[*Pause.*]

GUS: So fucking brilliant!

STU: The shower of wanks.

GUS: So they must've seen us waving Shuggie's ma's sheets.

STU: The headbangers.

GUS: Fucking ace.

STU: The headbanging Boys' Brigade bampots.

GUS: The Boys' Brigade are coming to get us.

STU: Because I only wanted to meet Shuggie's ma.

[*Pause.*]

GUS: So, Stu.

STU: What, Gus?

GUS: Come we'll climb down Shuggie's ma's sheets *now*?

STU: No.

GUS: And make 'the getaway'.

STU: *Oh* no.

GUS: No?

STU: No.

GUS: Aw.

Politics in the Park

Characters

JINTY Sixty-five
EFFIE Sixty-three

Setting

Park bench, Glasgow.

Politics in the Park was first performed as *Telling You the Laugh* at the Liverpool Playhouse Studio on 9 July 1986 with the following cast:

JINTY	*Sheila Donald*
EFFIE	*Anne Myatt*

Director: Tony Mulholland
Designer: Candida Boyes

Politics in the Park was first performed under that title at the Royal Lyceum Studio, Edinburgh, on 11 August 1987 with the following cast:

JINTY	*Sheila Donald*
EFFIE	*Sheila Latimer*

Director: Brian Ellsley

One: What's Gorgeous?

JINTY *and* EFFIE *are found on. They put down their bags.*

JINTY: This is lovely.
EFFIE: Aye.
JINTY: This is lovely, so it is.
EFFIE: Aye.
JINTY: Isn't it?
EFFIE: Aye . . . right enough.

[*Pause.*]

JINTY: Right enough what?
EFFIE: What?
JINTY: Right enough what?
EFFIE: Och . . . *right enough, right enough!*
JINTY: Tut.
EFFIE: Oh, right enough: it's gorgeous!

[*Pause.*]

JINTY: Aye, isn't it . . . ? What's gorgeous?
EFFIE: 'What's gorgeous?'
JINTY: Aye, what's gorgeous?
EFFIE: *My bum's* gorgeous.

[*Pause.*]

JINTY: You're all terrible to me.
EFFIE: Not at all.
JINTY: Aye. You all take a rise out of me.
EFFIE: Never.
JINTY: You all take a rise out of me, *something terrible.*
EFFIE: Oh no.
JINTY: You do so. Something, rotten.
EFFIE: Who does?
JINTY: The whole damned lot of you.

[*Pause.*]

EFFIE: You said a bad word.

JINTY: I did not.

EFFIE: Aye: your arse *did not.*

JINTY: Aye: *you* just said a bad word. (More like.)

EFFIE: *I'll tell your man* you said a bad word.

JINTY: Don't you dare. I'll tell *your* man *you* said a bad word.

EFFIE: Jinty.

JINTY: What, Effie?

EFFIE: My man couldn't care less if I say a bad word.

[*Pause.*]

JINTY: That's terrible, so it is.

EFFIE: *What's terrible?*

JINTY: Your man not minding if you say a bad word.

EFFIE: Och. You get used to it.

JINTY: I didn't know your man didn't mind if you say a bad word.

EFFIE: You get used to it, over the years.

[*Pause.*]

But, Jinty.

JINTY: What, Effie?

EFFIE: We *don't* take a rise out of you.

JINTY: You do.

EFFIE: No.

JINTY: You do. Aye. Because nobody . . .

EFFIE: Nobody what?

JINTY: Nobody . . .

EFFIE: Nobody *what*?

JINTY: Nobody . . . I can't remember.

[*Pause.*]

EFFIE: If you tell me what you were going to tell me, I won't tell your man you said a bad word.

JINTY: What? (Bad besom.)

EFFIE: Because your man minds if you say a bad word.
JINTY: I know. And Effie.
EFFIE: What, Jinty?
JINTY: Thank God my man minds if I say a bad word.

[*Pause.*]

EFFIE: But tell me what you were going to tell me and I won't tell your man you said a bad word.
JINTY: Promise.
EFFIE: Promise what?
JINTY: Promise not to tell my man I said a bad word.
EFFIE: So you admit you said a bad word? (Imagine saying a bad word.)
JINTY: You're too fly.
EFFIE: Right . . . I'm waiting.
JINTY: Too fly . . . Nobody – (You'll make a fool of me.)
EFFIE: No.
JINTY: You *always* make a fool of me.
EFFIE: Not at all . . . go on.
JINTY: I'm going on. Nobody –
EFFIE: Oh, for God's sake. Are you going to tell me what you were going to tell me?
JINTY: All right. All right, Nobody, nobody, nobody loves me. Nobody!

[*Pause.*]

What's up?
EFFIE: Nothing.
JINTY: You sure?

[EFFIE *laughs.*]

I knew it.

[EFFIE *laughs.*]

Is that you laughing at me?
EFFIE: [*Laughing*] No.

JINTY: I *knew* you'd laugh at me.

EFFIE: [*Laughing*] No, no, no, 'Nobody loves me.'

JINTY: I get made a fool of. I always get made a fool of. Nobody loves me!

[EFFIE *stops laughing.*]

EFFIE: You're right, Jinty.

JINTY: What about, Effie?

EFFIE: Nobody loves you.

JINTY: That's a terrible thing to say to your sister.

Two: Watching My Time

JINTY: I'll need to watch my time.
EFFIE: We're not long here.
JINTY: I'll need to watch my time, all the same.
EFFIE: We're not long here!
JINTY: Because I've got visitors coming.
EFFIE: We're not long here, neither we are. (Visitors?)
JINTY: Visitors!
EFFIE: I thought you weren't having any.
JINTY: Well, it's my man's sisters.
EFFIE: You get a rise taken out of you.

[*Pause.*]

JINTY: I'll have to watch my time, all the same.
EFFIE: You told me you were going to stop having visitors.
JINTY: I know.
EFFIE: Here you are having visitors.
JINTY: I know.
EFFIE: It's not right.
JINTY: Och, I know.
EFFIE: You'll get ill.
JINTY: I know, I know.
EFFIE: You'll end up with a stroke.
JINTY: Och –
EFFIE: Och what?
JINTY: Och you exaggerate.

[*Pause.*]

EFFIE: Are you not enjoying yourself?
JINTY: Did you ask if I'm not enjoying myself?
EFFIE: Aye, I did.
JINTY: Well imagine asking if I'm enjoying myself. That's a terrible thing to ask. 'Am I enjoying myself?' *Of course* I'm enjoying myself.

EFFIE: I thought maybe the company wasn't good enough for you.

JINTY: How could you think the company might not be good enough for me?

EFFIE: I just thought it . . . Because I thought we were here for the afternoon.

JINTY: We are.

EFFIE: Not that it matters.

JINTY: We *are* here for the afternoon. I've just got to watch my time.

EFFIE: Listen to it.

JINTY: And you know what you're like.

EFFIE: What 'I'm' like. This is pathetic.

JINTY: You could talk for a whole afternoon.

EFFIE: Pathetic, so it is.

JINTY: For a whole afternoon, so you could. And you know what *I'm* like –

EFFIE: I am not a talker.

JINTY: I'm soft enough to let you.

EFFIE: Not a talker, neither I am.

JINTY: Soft enough to let you, so I am.

EFFIE: Your arse is soft enough to let me.

JINTY: Sssshhh.

EFFIE: Sssshhh yourself. Sssshhh what for?

JINTY: You said a bad word in a loud voice. Your loud voice will carry in the wind.

EFFIE: Your arse will carry in the wind.

[*Pause.*]

JINTY: I'm not with you.

EFFIE: Fine.

JINTY: If anyone comes over to check us, because you said a bad word, I'm saying I'm not with you.

EFFIE: And I'll say, 'See my old mother here.'

JINTY: Besom.

EFFIE: I'll say, 'See my old mother here: she's not all right in the head.'

JINTY: Aye, and I wouldn't put it past you.

[*Pause.*]

I'm only saying I'll have to watch my time.

EFFIE: *Are* you enjoying yourself?

JINTY: What? Of course I'm enjoying myself. I like it here. You get a view. I'd like to paint it. I'll paint it some day.

[*Short pause.*]

EFFIE: But the company's just not good enough for you?

JINTY: Tut. Och see you. Just stop it. And anyway: *you've* got to get back for *your* man's tea.

EFFIE: I know.

JINTY: *You'll* have to watch *your* time too.

EFFIE: Aye, I know.

JINTY: Good. Well you can just hold that tongue of yours in future. A piece of nonsense talking like that. (I mean to say: if it hadn't been for your man's tea, you could've come back and had your tea with me.) Do you *want* to come back and have tea with me?

EFFIE: I've got *my* man's tea to get back to.

JINTY: Oh well, then.

EFFIE: Thanks.

Three: Catching the City Bakeries

JINTY: And I'll have to catch the City Bakeries.

EFFIE: Oh.

JINTY: Yes, I'll have to catch the City Bakeries, before they close.

EFFIE: What'll you have to catch the City Bakeries for?

JINTY: Because the City Bakeries shuts early on a Tuesday.

[*Pause.*]

EFFIE: Aye, but what'll you have to catch the City Bakeries for?

JINTY: They do nice Princess cakes in the City Bakeries.

EFFIE: I *know* they do nice Princess cakes. But what do you want nice Princess cakes *for*?

JINTY: For my visitors.

[*Pause.*]

EFFIE: You don't need to go to all that bother.

JINTY: Och it's no bother.

EFFIE: All the stuff you bake, too.

JINTY: People have got to have something to eat.

EFFIE: And you end up throwing half of it out.

JINTY: And what is that supposed to mean? (You're too cheeky.)

EFFIE: You bake far too much.

JINTY: Not really.

EFFIE: Come off it.

JINTY: Most of it gets eaten.

EFFIE: How often do you do a baking?

JINTY: Every morning.

EFFIE: See what I mean? Damned ridiculous.

JINTY: Well, it gets eaten.

EFFIE: There's only two of you, too.

JINTY: My visitors get some. My daughter gets some. (I take it to her.) *You* get some.

EFFIE: Aye. Stop bringing me so much.

JINTY: I thought you liked it.

EFFIE: I do like it.

JINTY: And your man likes it.

EFFIE: Aye, but you do too much. Sometimes you do too much.

JINTY: I thought you liked it.

EFFIE: I like it.

JINTY: I'll not bother giving you any more.

EFFIE: I'm not saying that.

JINTY: I can take a hint. You put my good baking in the bin, I bet.

EFFIE: Not at all.

JINTY: You probably put it in the bin.

EFFIE: Only very occasionally.

JINTY: My good baking! That's a waste!

EFFIE: Only if you give me too much.

JINTY: A waste of my good baking.

EFFIE: I didn't mean that.

JINTY: I'm up every morning baking.

EFFIE: ⎫ No wonder you're exhausted.
JINTY: ⎭ No wonder I'm exhausted.

   [*Pause.*]

EFFIE: And I *don't* throw out your baking.

JINTY: So why did you say you throw out my baking?

EFFIE: Och I'll say anything. (You know what I'm like.) I'll say anything to keep you going. I like to keep you going.

JINTY: Aye. You like to take a rise out of me. Don't you?

   [*Pause.*]

   Don't you? (The whole damned lot of you.) Don't you?

EFFIE: I heard you.

JINTY: Why didn't you answer?

EFFIE: I was thinking. Am I allowed to think?

JINTY: Aye: you're aye thinking. Thinking bad thoughts about your sister likely.

EFFIE: Och never.

JINTY: Thinking bad thoughts about your sister's baking likely.

EFFIE: There's not a thing wrong with your baking, except —

JINTY: Aye and that *will* be right. You haven't got a good word to say about my baking . . . Except what?

EFFIE: What?

JINTY: Except what?

EFFIE: Except it's not as good as mines's.

[*Pause.*]

You made me say it.

JINTY: You don't bake.

EFFIE: Aye, but when I *do* bake.

JINTY: There's no point in saying this.

EFFIE: When I do bake, people say it's smashing.

JINTY: You *never* bake.

EFFIE: When I do bake, people prefer it to yours.

JINTY: Imagine saying that.

EFFIE: People always say my baking's smashing.

JINTY: You're making all this up.

EFFIE: No.

JINTY: And I wouldn't put it past you. And. I do a lovely baking. People pass complimentary remarks about my baking . . . Do you think I should stop baking? I'm going to stop baking.

EFFIE: Och, why?

JINTY: I do too much.

EFFIE: Pay no attention to me.

JINTY: My visitors take a rise out of me.

EFFIE: I'm a pain in the neck.

JINTY: I never get invited back to theirs.

EFFIE: I talk a load of tripe.

JINTY: And if I *do* get invited back to theirs, I'm lucky if I get a crummy slice of toast and a pancake.

[*Short pause.*]

EFFIE: Cut the visitors down.
JINTY: My visitors can all go to hell.
EFFIE: Quite right.
JINTY: They can all go to hell, after tonight. And Effie.
EFFIE: What, Jinty?
JINTY: Are you ready for something to eat yet?

[*Pause. They pick up their bags.*]

Four: A Generation with a Lot of Go

They put down their bags. EFFIE *picks her bag back up and starts to rummage in it.*

JINTY: Have you not had enough to eat *yet*?
EFFIE: That was a lovely picnic.

> [EFFIE *produces an opened blue airmail letter.*]

JINTY: But *have* you not had enough to eat yet?
EFFIE: And I could just do it again.

> [EFFIE *handles the letter slightly ostentatiously, and* JINTY *observes the ostentatious handling covertly.*]

JINTY: So you enjoyed it?
EFFIE: The same again would go down well.
JINTY: As long as you enjoyed it.
EFFIE: All the same.
JINTY: That's the main thing.

> [EFFIE *puts the letter in a side compartment and puts her bag down.*]

JINTY: You are awful greedy, Effie. Because enough's enough.
EFFIE: I've got a healthy appetite on me, *just like my boy.*

> [*Pause.*]

JINTY: Och a boy's different.
EFFIE: Not at all.
JINTY: A big appetite's understandable in a boy.
EFFIE: I'm the picture of health. (Unlike some people.)

> [*Pause.*]

JINTY: And what is that supposed to mean?
EFFIE: Nothing.

JINTY: Because my health's been not too bad.
EFFIE: A lot of garbage you talk.
JINTY: Not too bad at all recently.
EFFIE: And let's face it, Jinty.
JINTY: What, Effie?
EFFIE: You're half dead already.

[*Pause.*]

JINTY: I'm not going to bother with you.
EFFIE: Good.
JINTY: I'm just not going to bother with you, in future.
EFFIE: I'll be glad to see the back of you.
JINTY: You go too far.
EFFIE: Just because I've got a sense of humour.
JINTY: You go too far with your sense of humour.
EFFIE: Just because you can't take a sense of humour.
JINTY: So I'm not going to bother with you, in future.
EFFIE: Fine.

[*Long pause.*]

JINTY: But, Effie.
EFFIE: What, Jinty? (I knew you couldn't keep it up.)
JINTY: Och see you: you're too fly: you *knew* I couldn't keep it up.

[*Pause.*]

EFFIE: So what was it you wanted?
JINTY: Och it's not important.
EFFIE: Come on.
JINTY: Och it doesn't matter.
EFFIE: Fine.

[*Pause.*]

JINTY: But, Effie.
EFFIE: What, Jinty?
JINTY: What was that I saw you with?

EFFIE: Where?

JINTY: Was that *a letter* I saw you with?

EFFIE: When?

JINTY: (By the way.)

EFFIE: Me?

JINTY: I'm sure I saw you with a letter.

EFFIE: Well, if I had a letter —

JINTY: And I just wondered about it.

EFFIE: If I had a letter, *it was none of your damned business.*

[*Pause.*]

JINTY: You had a letter in your bag.

EFFIE: Have you *been in* my bag?

JINTY: You brought the letter out your bag.

EFFIE: Because just stay out of my bag.

JINTY: You held it up a wee minute.

EFFIE: Stay out of my bag the next time.

JINTY: And then you put it back in your bag.

EFFIE: And Jinty.

JINTY: What, Effie?

EFFIE: Just keep your beady eyes to yourself, in future.

[*Pause.*]

JINTY: So was the letter from your boy?

EFFIE: How come you think it was from my boy?

JINTY: I just wondered.

[*Pause.*]

EFFIE: That must have been an awful close look you took.

JINTY: I *just wondered* if it was from your boy.

EFFIE: An *awful close* look you took.

JINTY: Because I couldn't help noticing it was an airmail letter.

EFFIE: And my boy's doing fine.

JINTY: An airmail letter from *abroad.*

EFFIE: And it's awful good of my boy: hitch-hiking round Europe —

JINTY: And what did he want in it?

EFFIE: Hitch-hiking round Europe and still takes time to write to his mother.

   [*Pause.*]

JINTY: But what did your boy *want* in the letter?

EFFIE: Never you mind what my boy wanted.

JINTY: Och your boy probably wanted a few bob –

EFFIE: At least my boy took the time to write to his mother.

JINTY: Probably just wanted a few bob, if I know your boy.

EFFIE: And what if my boy *did* want a few bob?

JINTY: Well my boy doesn't write and ask me for money.

EFFIE: And do you know why that is, Jinty?

JINTY: Why, Effie?

EFFIE: It's because your boy doesn't write to you *at all*.

   [*Pause.*]

JINTY: Of course, my boy's got a *career*.

EFFIE: A selfish eedyit that boy of yours. (A career?)

JINTY: A career and *a family*.

EFFIE: Oh 'a family'! Well at least my boy's got his *independence*.

JINTY: At least my boy's got his *security*.

EFFIE: At least my boy's got his *freedom*.

JINTY: At least my boy's a – a – a *commuter*.

   [*Pause.*]

   Yes. At least my boy's to commute to *New York City* every day.

EFFIE: Well your boy deserves to be – New York City?

JINTY: Yes. Commutes to New York City every day for his –

EFFIE: Aye. 'New York City.' A violent hell-hole of a place that place.

JINTY: Commutes to New York City every day for his *career*.

EFFIE: A violent – But for not writing to his mother your boy *deserves to be shot*.

[*Pause.*]

Because imagine not writing.
JINTY: At least my boy doesn't go hitch-hiking.
EFFIE: Imagine not writing to his mother.
JINTY: Imagine hitch-hiking round Europe.

[*Pause.*]

Aye, what's your boy hitch-hiking round Europe for?
EFFIE: Och they're all at it these days.
JINTY: Imagine hitch-hiking round Europe.
EFFIE: As a generation they have a lot of go in them.
JINTY: A piece of nonsense.
EFFIE: More go in them than you or I.

[*Pause.*]

JINTY: And *whereabouts* in Europe's your boy hitch-hiking *to*?
EFFIE: Everywhere.
JINTY: Everywhere?
EFFIE: Aye. (The lot.)
JINTY: To France, Italy and Switzerland?
EFFIE: Och aye.
JINTY: To Spain, Belgium and Czechoslovakia?
EFFIE: Aye. (There's no holding him back.)
JINTY: And Germany? He's going to Germany too, I suppose?
EFFIE: Germany? Of course Germany. The lot, I said.
JINTY: Well he *shouldn't* be.
EFFIE: (Are you going deaf or something?)
JINTY: He shouldn't *be* going to Germany.
EFFIE: And why not?
JINTY: He just shouldn't!

Five: Painting the View

EFFIE: So when *are* you going to paint the view?
JINTY: What?
EFFIE: You said you were going to paint the view.
JINTY: Och I'll paint the view when I'm ready.

[*Pause.*]

EFFIE: Because you'll have to watch what time of day you paint the view.
JINTY: I know.
EFFIE: Because the wrong time of day and you'll *not get* much of a view.
JINTY: I know I'll have to watch the time of day I paint the view.
EFFIE: Not much of a view *to paint*.
JINTY: Because I'd need to get the light.
EFFIE: Because there's a lot of rape around.
JINTY: I'd need to come early to get the light.
EFFIE: There's a wave of rapes and muggings in the park.
JINTY: Yes. I'd need to – (What?)
EFFIE: So if you got raped or mugged in the park, the only view you'd get's the inside of a hospital.
JINTY: Och –
EFFIE: (If you're lucky.)

[*Pause.*]

But you could always get someone to –
JINTY: I would just get someone to –
EFFIE: You could always get someone to –
JINTY: ⎫ Just get someone to *come with me*.
EFFIE: ⎭ Always get someone to *come with you*.

[*Pause.*]

EFFIE: So who could you get to come with you?

JINTY: I don't know.
EFFIE: Do you think?
JINTY: I'm not sure.
EFFIE: You could get your wee man to come with you.
JINTY: My wee man's working early.

[*Pause.*]

EFFIE: *I* could always come with you.
JINTY: If you came, *I* wouldn't come.
EFFIE: I could always come with you, so I could.
JINTY: I couldn't paint the view if you came, Effie.
EFFIE: Why not, Jinty?
JINTY: You talk too much.

[*Pause.*]

EFFIE: You've no right to say that.
JINTY: What?
EFFIE: No right to say I talk too much.
JINTY: Tut . . . Och *that's* what you meant.

[*Dialogue overlaps. Italic speech takes precedence.*]

EFFIE: *And if I do talk a lot.*
JINTY: Because that's *not what I meant.*
EFFIE: If I do have *a lively personality.*
JINTY: I just meant I *couldn't paint the view.*
EFFIE: *That's why I'm very popular at parties.*
JINTY: I just meant I *couldn't work if I get interrupted.*
EFFIE: That's why I'm *very popular at parties.*
JINTY: And let's face it: *you would interrupt me.*

[*Pause.*]

EFFIE: *I remember at* my mother's funeral.
JINTY: And *I'm not trying to blame you for interrupting me.*
EFFIE: At my mother's funeral ceremony, *I had everyone laughing.*

JINTY: Yes, that was shameful.
EFFIE: I'm the cheerful type.

JINTY: I was ashamed of you.

EFFIE: I'm very forward-looking.

JINTY: Someone should've stopped you –

EFFIE: That's why I'm popular.

JINTY: Someone should've stopped you –

EFFIE: I mean: I know my wee man didn't turn up to my mother's funeral.

[*Pause.*]

[*Dialogue overlaps. Italic speech takes precedence.*]

JINTY: *Och your wee man should've turned up and stopped you* having everyone laughing at my mother's funeral.

EFFIE: *Even if my wee man had turned up, he wouldn't've stopped me having everyone laughing.*

JINTY: Yes, your wee man should've turned up and stopped you *at my mother's funeral.*

[*Pause.*]

JINTY: *So I'm not going to bother painting the view.*

EFFIE: Yes, I'm glad I'm *the cheerful type.*

JINTY: No, I'm not going to bother *painting the view.*

EFFIE: Yes, I'm glad I'm *popular at parties.*

Six: Farting

Long pause. EFFIE *slaps her leg. Pause.* EFFIE *again slaps her leg.*

JINTY: Och. What is it?
EFFIE: What's what?
JINTY: You slapped your leg.
EFFIE: When?
JINTY: Just now.
EFFIE: Your arse.
JINTY: What?
EFFIE: Your arse slapped my leg.

[*Pause.* EFFIE *slaps her leg.*]

JINTY: Well I heard you *that time.*
EFFIE: No.
JINTY: I did . . . God, anyone would think you were passing
wind.
EFFIE: What? When?
JINTY: I think you passed wind.
EFFIE: Me pass wind? Are you trying to say I would fart?
JINTY: Sssshhh.
EFFIE: You're saying I farted.
JINTY: Sssshhh. (I don't want a showing up.)
EFFIE: What with?
JINTY: I don't want a showing up with you saying *that word.*
EFFIE: Fart?
JINTY: You saying that word, *in an awful loud voice.*
EFFIE: *What word?*
JINTY: *That* word.
EFFIE: *Tell me* what word.
JINTY: *I'm* not saying it.

[*Pause.*]

Did you slap your leg to cover it up? Did you? You did.

[EFFIE *controls an impulse to laugh.*]

What is it? You laughing?

EFFIE: Not at all.

JINTY: You're laughing.

EFFIE: No, no. [*Laughs.*] Cheeky besom. Imagine noticing. Wait till I tell your man that one. Wait till I tell him you caught me farting. Wait till I tell him you caught me slapping my leg to cover it up. Anyone would think you never farted.

JINTY: I don't.

EFFIE: You do.

JINTY: I don't. (What a conversation.)

EFFIE: I've heard you.

JINTY: What? Where?

EFFIE: I've *heard* you.

JINTY: I don't think so.

EFFIE: In the kitchen, making the dinner. Farting your head off.

JINTY: No.

EFFIE: Yes. Wee high-pitched ones. Like a whistle.

[*She mimics the sound.* JINTY *controls an impulse to laugh.*]

What is it?

JINTY: Nothing.

EFFIE: No. What is it?

JINTY: Nothing.

EFFIE: You laughing? You're laughing.

[JINTY *laughs.*]

I knew it. My sister's laughing. What was so funny?

JINTY: I didn't know you knew.

EFFIE: What?

JINTY: You know.

EFFIE: Tell me.

JINTY: I fart while I'm peeling the potatoes.

EFFIE: That's disgusting.

JINTY: Peeling the potatoes seems to bring it out of me.

EFFIE: Aye, you'll have to try and control this farting while you're peeling the potatoes.

JINTY: I can't help it. I peel the potatoes and I fart. They belong together.

[*Pause.*]

EFFIE: Aye, and do you know something, Jinty?

JINTY: What, Effie?

EFFIE: Farting runs in the family.

Seven: The Soft Touch

EFFIE: Jinty, gorgeous.
JINTY: What, Effie, dear?
EFFIE: You got thirty pounds you can lend your wee sister?
JINTY: Thirty pounds?
EFFIE: Thirty pounds.

[*Short pause.*]

JINTY: I suppose you're thinking I'm a soft touch.
EFFIE: Not at all.
JINTY: Because my wee man's never done giving me into a row.
EFFIE: Kind and generous, yes. Soft, never.
JINTY: Never done giving me into a row for being a soft touch.
EFFIE: Definitely not a soft touch.

[*Pause.*]

EFFIE: So, Jinty, gorgeous.
JINTY: What, Effie, dear?
EFFIE: You *got* thirty pounds you can lend your wee sister?
JINTY: Effie.
EFFIE: What, Jinty?
JINTY: If my wee sister needs thirty pounds, I'll lend her thirty pounds.

[*Pause.*]

EFFIE: It's helluva big of you, Jinty.
JINTY: Don't mention it, Effie.
EFFIE: You're a wonderful woman, right enough.

[JINTY *laughs.*]

Oh aye. (I don't deserve you.)
JINTY: [*Laughing*] Sssshhh.
EFFIE: I *don't.*

JINTY: [*Laughing*] Sssshhh.

EFFIE: I mean: even as a child —

JINTY: [*Laughing*] No. Sssshhh.

EFFIE: Aye. Even as a child, I used to batter you stupid.

[*Pause.* JINTY *stops laughing.*]

JINTY: Och I know!

EFFIE: Batter you stupid, so I did.

JINTY: I know. And I was daft enough to let you.

EFFIE: Yes, you were daft enough to let me. (Imagine *letting* someone batter you stupid.)

JINTY: I must've been stupid.

EFFIE: You *were* stupid.

JINTY: There was that one time, though.

EFFIE: I know.

JINTY: That one time you battered me.

EFFIE: That one time I battered you stupid.

JINTY: You battered me and I lifted my hand to batter you back.

EFFIE: You lifted your hand to batter me back.

JINTY: And Mrs Campbell opened her kitchenette window and shouted, 'Jinty Baird! Jinty Baird! If I see you lifting your hand to batter your wee sister *again*, I'll go right round and tell your mother.'

[*Pause.*]

EFFIE: That must have been terrible for you.

JINTY: Terrible! Mrs Campbell closed her window again before I could even answer her back.

EFFIE: I felt sorry for you.

JINTY: Did you, Effie?

EFFIE: You'd lifted your hand for nothing.

[*Pause.*]

EFFIE: When can I get this thirty pounds, Jinty?

JINTY: So when do you *want* this thirty pounds, Effie?

EFFIE: As soon as you can find it in your heart to give it to your wee sister.

[*Pause.*]

JINTY: So what's this thirty pounds for?
EFFIE: Does it matter?
JINTY: (Not that it matters.)
EFFIE: So don't ask.
JINTY: So I won't ask.

[*Pause.*]

But this thirty pounds's not for your boy, is it?
EFFIE: You said you wouldn't ask.
JINTY: Och I couldn't help asking.
EFFIE: Didn't you?
JINTY: Could I?

[*Pause.*]

JINTY: And why did you not ask your wee man for the thirty pounds, Effie?
EFFIE: Och —
JINTY: Because I don't understand your wee man.
EFFIE: Och you'd get used to him.
JINTY: I doubt if I'd get used to him.
EFFIE: You'd get used to him — the bad wee tight-fisted eedyit — over the years.
JINTY: Because my wee man isn't the least bit tight-fisted.
EFFIE: So you would.
JINTY: Neither he is.

[*Pause.*]

EFFIE: So, Jinty.
JINTY: What, Effie?
EFFIE: *Thanks* for the lend of the thirty pounds.

Eight: Telling You the Laugh

EFFIE: So did I tell you the laugh?

JINTY: What laugh was that?

EFFIE: Do you *want* to hear the laugh? It's nothing –

JINTY: I hope it's nothing dirty.

EFFIE: It's nothing dirty.

JINTY: Because I could just *go* a good laugh.

EFFIE: Well, it's nothing dirty.

JINTY: Yes, I hope it's nothing dirty.

EFFIE: What gave you the idea –?

JINTY: Because your tongue's –

EFFIE: What gave you the idea it could be something dirty?

JINTY: Because your tongue's terrible sometimes.

[*Pause.*]

EFFIE: I know: my tongue's terrible sometimes!

JINTY: So what about this laugh?

EFFIE: What?

JINTY: The laugh you were going to tell me.

EFFIE: Oh aye. Aye. The laugh I was going to tell you!

[*Pause.*]

My wee man's Aunty Jessie died.

JINTY: That's not funny.

EFFIE: What? *What's* not funny?

JINTY: Your wee man's Aunty Jessie dying isn't funny.

EFFIE: Of course *that's* not funny.

JINTY: You told me it was going to be funny.

EFFIE: Because that's not *the funny bit*.

JINTY: And I could've just gone a good laugh too. (What?)

EFFIE: *Not* the funny bit.

[*Short pause.*]

JINTY: So *tell me* the funny bit.

EFFIE: Well, remember that time I stayed at yours for a few
   days after your operation?

JINTY: Aye.

EFFIE: And I was exhausted from helping you.

JINTY: Aye.

EFFIE: Because you were a bad impatient besom of a patient.

JINTY: Aye. No! I wasn't. (It's to be expected.)

EFFIE: You were.

JINTY: Well!

EFFIE: Well what?

JINTY: Well, how would *you* like to spend a few days recuper-
   ating from an operation?

EFFIE: A bad impatient besom, right enough.

JINTY: You could try to be nice –

EFFIE: So I stayed at yours for a few days –

JINTY: You could try to be nice –

EFFIE: I stayed at yours for a few days and I got a taxi home.

JINTY: Try to be nice about it. (A taxi?)

EFFIE: *A taxi home!*

JINTY: What did you get a taxi home for?

EFFIE: I was exhausted.

JINTY: No need to get a taxi.

EFFIE: You were a bad impatient besom of a patient!

JINTY: Damned extravagance.

EFFIE: So I got a taxi home.

JINTY: Will you hurry up and tell me the laugh –

EFFIE: So I *had to* get a taxi home.

JINTY: And stop calling me a bad impatient besom.

EFFIE: So I got in the house – (You were – a bad impatient
   besom.)

[JINTY *starts to interrupt.*]

So! So, I got in the house . . . ! And there's my wee man
standing in his Sunday best. I says, 'Where are you going?'
He says, 'My Aunty Jessie's dead.' I said, 'Why didn't you
come to Jinty's and tell me?' He said, 'Och.' I said, 'When is

it?' He said, 'The now.' I said, 'I would like to have gone to your Aunty Jessie's funeral.' He said, 'Och.' I said, 'But I'm not dressed for a funeral.' He said, 'It's *too late* to get dressed.' I said, 'You could've at least come to Jinty's and told me there was a funeral on.' He said – (Do you know what he said?) – He said, 'Who the bloody hell cares whether you go to my Aunty Jessie's funeral or not?' So the laugh. [*Laughs.*] I laughed.

[*She stops laughing. Pause.*]

JINTY: *That's* not funny.
EFFIE: Well, I think it's funny.
JINTY: Definitely not funny.
EFFIE: Why don't you think it's funny?
JINTY: Because if my wee man had an Aunty Jessie, he'd *want me* to go to her funeral.

Nine: Growing Up Cheeky

JINTY: Well.

EFFIE: Well what?

JINTY: 'Well what?' Have you enjoyed yourself? (I *hope* you've enjoyed yourself.)

EFFIE: Oh I've enjoyed *my*self, right enough.

JINTY: The very least you could've done is enjoy yourself.

EFFIE: I've enjoyed myself and shut up.

[*Pause.*]

JINTY: You're too cheeky.

EFFIE: I know.

JINTY: I've always had to take a lot of cheek off you.

EFFIE: And you've always *deserved* the cheek you've had off me.

JINTY: See you.

EFFIE: You've deserved it. Trailing through life, your arse hanging out your frock like that.

JINTY: Och it is not.

EFFIE: It is. The arse hanging out the frock.

JINTY: No.

EFFIE: Aye.

JINTY: No . . . Aye? Why didn't you tell me? Why didn't you tell me my arse was hanging out my frock. See: you make me wild. Look what you've made me say. And my arse probably *isn't* hanging out my frock.

EFFIE: Aye.

[*Pause.*]

Aye. Your arse isn't hanging out your frock. (And shut up.)

[*Short pause.*]

JINTY: Well what did you say it was for?

EFFIE: Och I just said it and to hell. (I'm cheeky.)

JINTY: Aye. You're cheeky.

EFFIE: I've *always* been cheeky.

JINTY: You've always *been* cheeky. You'll need to try and change.

EFFIE: I always will be cheeky.

JINTY: And I don't know *who* you take it from.

EFFIE: My cheek?

JINTY: Your cheek: you don't take it from me.

EFFIE: I know. You're polite. Not from *you*.

JINTY: Who from, then?

EFFIE: From my old father.

JINTY: You didn't take it from *my* old father.

EFFIE: Aye.

JINTY: *My* old father wasn't cheeky.

EFFIE: My old father was *renowned* for his cheek.

JINTY: No.

EFFIE: He told the boss's wife to get stuffed.

JINTY: Oh. Now he did not tell the boss's wife to get stuffed.

EFFIE: He did. And I take after him: if I had a boss's wife, I'd tell her to get stuffed.

JINTY: Oh you would not.

EFFIE: Aye. Because I took after my old father. In fact: I took after my old father *deliberately*.

JINTY: No.

EFFIE: Because I didn't want to end up polite all my days.

JINTY: Imagine growing up cheeky *deliberately*.

EFFIE: Neither I didn't.

JINTY: That's shocking behaviour.

EFFIE: Did I?

[*Pause.*]

JINTY: But you were always my father's favourite.

EFFIE: Aye.

JINTY: You were spoilt.

EFFIE: Aye.

JINTY: You always got anything good that was going.

EFFIE: *Oh* aye.

JINTY: And I got left with nothing.

EFFIE: Aye, right enough.

JINTY: 'Aye, right enough.' You shouldn't be agreeing. You should be apologizing and making it up to your sister.

EFFIE: Aye . . . Jinty.

JINTY: What, Effie?

EFFIE: Did you enjoy your childhood?

JINTY: What? What kind of question is that to ask? That's a terrible question to ask. Why do you ask?

EFFIE: Och I just wondered. Did you?

JINTY: No, I didn't . . . ! I was always ill.

EFFIE: That was a shame.

JINTY: I was never out my sickbed, *as you well know*. So why do you ask?

EFFIE: Why did I ask if you enjoyed your childhood?

JINTY: Yes, why did you ask if I enjoyed my childhood?

EFFIE: Because I enjoyed *mine*.

Ten: The Peroxide Blonde Bitch

Pause. EFFIE *sees something.*

JINTY: Well, Effie . . .

EFFIE: We can't go yet, Jinty . . .

JINTY: I've got to – Why not?

EFFIE: Look what's over there first.

JINTY: (I've got *to go*.) Where?

EFFIE: It's the peroxide blonde bitch.

> [JINTY *goes to look, but changes her mind.*]

JINTY: Eh, I think we'll go now. Because you shouldn't be –

EFFIE: And I told you about her.

JINTY: You shouldn't be –

EFFIE: Aye: it's the peroxide blonde bitch –

JINTY: You shouldn't be *staring* at a 'peroxide blonde bitch'.

EFFIE: It's the peroxide blonde bitch has slept with every wee man in – staring?

JINTY: Well, she hasn't slept with *my* wee man.

EFFIE: I'll stare where I – Och *who'd* sleep with your wee man?

JINTY: Oh now, that's not very –

EFFIE: Your wee man's got a nose like –

JINTY: Not very –

EFFIE: Your wee man's got a face like –

JINTY: Not very –

EFFIE: Your wee man's got a personality like a plate of tripe. (What?)

JINTY: Not very *nice*.

EFFIE: Oh *aye*: sorry.

JINTY: Not very nice *at all*.

EFFIE: I mean: *awful* sorry. Because your wee man's the nicest wee man in –

JINTY: What? Oh I know he is.

EFFIE: The nicest wee man in –
JINTY: (The soul.)
EFFIE: But I'll stare where I *want to* stare.
JINTY: The soul! (What?)
EFFIE: And you won't stop me.

[EFFIE *looks out blatantly.* JINTY *looks puzzledly at* EFFIE, *then looks away sharply.*]

JINTY: And has your wee man slept with this 'peroxide blonde'?
EFFIE: Eh? Aye. Of course my wee man's slept with the peroxide blonde.
JINTY: Well imagine sleeping with a peroxide blonde. That's –
EFFIE: Because my wee man's –
JINTY: That's *terrible*.
EFFIE: My wee man's –
JINTY: Why didn't you tell me?
EFFIE: My wee man's tall, dark and distinguished-looking . . . (What?)
JINTY: Why didn't –?
EFFIE: Och I *did* tell you. Not remember I told you I caught him?
JINTY: Och now, that's not very nice. Imagine catching him. Where did you catch him?
EFFIE: I told you I caught him jumping out the peroxide blonde's bedroom window.
JINTY: Did he?
EFFIE: Och aye.
JINTY: What did he do that for?
EFFIE: Because I battered the peroxide blonde's front door.
JINTY: So what did he say?
EFFIE: When?
JINTY: When you caught him jumping out the peroxide blonde's bedroom window?
EFFIE: He said he was just helping her out with some repairs.

JINTY: And did you believe him?
EFFIE: I believed him.
JINTY: What did you believe him for?
EFFIE: Och I *didn't* believe him.
JINTY: What did you *say* you believed him for?
EFFIE: I was pulling your —
JINTY: Och.

[*She turns away.* EFFIE *takes this in and looks out.*]

So I think we'll go now.
EFFIE: What?
JINTY: We're going now.
EFFIE: No.
JINTY: We're going!
EFFIE: No!
JINTY: Right. What's going on?
EFFIE: We are waiting till that clears off out the park. Because we are not going near that. Are we?
JINTY: So I suppose we've to sit here all afternoon waiting for *that* to leave.
EFFIE: I —

[JINTY *has seen something.*]

JINTY: Now wait a wee minute.
EFFIE: What?
JINTY: Is that her?
EFFIE: Where?
JINTY: Is that her at the bowling green?

[EFFIE *looks out.*]

EFFIE: That's her.
JINTY: Because she's not much of a peroxide blonde *now*.
EFFIE: Eh? (Oh *aye*.)
JINTY: She's more of a mousy brown.
EFFIE: Hah. Aye. More of a dirty fair.
JINTY: More of a whity grey.

EFFIE: Aye. More of a half bald and more to come.

[*They laugh together.* EFFIE *comes out of it first.*]

And you shouldn't be –
JINTY: Eh? Oh I know. You've got me –
EFFIE: You shouldn't be –
JINTY: You've even got me –
EFFIE: You shouldn't be –
JINTY: }
EFFIE: } Staring.

[*They laugh together again. This time* JINTY *comes out of it first, renewing her stare.*]

JINTY: And is that the one . . . ?
EFFIE: What?
JINTY: Is she the one . . . ?
EFFIE: *What?*
JINTY: Is she the one you said you'd walk right past, next time you saw her in the street?
EFFIE: That's the one.
JINTY: I remember now.
EFFIE: (God.)
JINTY: Well why don't we walk right past her *now*?
EFFIE: I've already walked right past her once.
JINTY: When?
EFFIE: August 1961. Two weeks after I caught my wee man jumping out her bedroom window.

[*Pause.*]

JINTY: So do you not fancy walking right past her *again*?
EFFIE: No.
JINTY: Why not?
EFFIE: I don't bear grudges.
JINTY: I don't blame you.
EFFIE: Besides, it's too late.
JINTY: Oh *why*?
EFFIE: She's just walked out the park.

Eleven: Germans

JINTY: We can go now, then?

EFFIE: Jinty.

JINTY: I *suppose* we can go now, then?

EFFIE: Jinty!

JINTY: What, Effie?

EFFIE: Aren't you forgetting something?

[*Pause.* JINTY *picks up her bag and takes out her purse. She goes to open it and changes her mind.*]

JINTY: But I hope your boy doesn't hitch-hike round Germany with my thirty pounds.

EFFIE: Och. What difference does it make?

JINTY: I don't like Germany.

EFFIE: What's wrong with Germany?

JINTY: Germans.

[*Pause.*]

EFFIE: You're too bitter.

JINTY: I am awful bitter.

EFFIE: And your memory's far too long.

JINTY: I'm bitter all right.

EFFIE: Far too long for your own good.

JINTY: And quite right too to be bitter.

[*Pause.*]

JINTY: A German killed my brother.

EFFIE: Och you don't know that.

JINTY: A German killed my brother.

EFFIE: (But I knew that was going to get brought up.)

JINTY: So who else could've killed my brother?

EFFIE: Anyone could've killed our brother.

JINTY: A German killed my brother.

EFFIE: An accident could've killed our brother.

JINTY: So don't you bother *letting that German off with it*.

[*Pause.*]

JINTY: So I think we'll just go now.
EFFIE: Aye but, Jinty, gorgeous.
JINTY: What, Effie, dear?
EFFIE: Can I get my thirty pounds first?

[*Pause.* JINTY *goes to open her purse and thinks better of it.*]

JINTY: So *is* your boy going to be hitch-hiking round Germany with that thirty pounds you're borrowing off me?
EFFIE: Jinty, gorgeous.
JINTY: What, Effie, dear?
EFFIE: Do you *have to* ask?
JINTY: I was only asking.
EFFIE: Because don't ask.

[JINTY *opens her purse and goes for the money and thinks better of it.*]

JINTY: So what was the postmark on that airmail letter?
EFFIE: Jinty.
JINTY: What, Effie?
EFFIE: Don't ask.

[*Pause.* JINTY *closes her purse emphatically. Pause.*]

EFFIE: So, Jinty!
JINTY: What, Effie?
EFFIE: Am I still getting the thirty pounds for my boy?

[*Pause.*]

JINTY: So the thirty pounds *is* for your boy!

[*Pause.*]

EFFIE: *Am I*, Jinty?
JINTY: Of course, Effie. *Of course* you're getting the thirty pounds for your boy.

EFFIE: Thanks.

[*She opens her purse.*]

JINTY: You're my sister.
EFFIE: Thanks.
JINTY: He's my nephew.

[JINTY *counts out three ten-pound notes and goes to hand it over.* EFFIE *gets ready to take it. Then* JINTY *thinks better of it and brings the money back.*]

JINTY: But you know what, Effie?
EFFIE: What, Jinty?
JINTY: I'm too damned soft a touch for my own good.
EFFIE: [*Mutters*] Aye. Right enough.

[JINTY *hands the money to* EFFIE, *who puts it in her purse. They close their purses and put them in their bags.*]

Twelve: I Will Have to Get Back

EFFIE: Well, *I've* enjoyed myself.

JINTY: Good.

EFFIE: I'm *still* enjoying myself.

JINTY: Good. Pleased to hear it. And so am I enjoying myself.

[*Pause.*]

But I will have to get back now.

EFFIE: Och.

JINTY: I'll have to.

EFFIE: Do you have to?

JINTY: I'll have to.

EFFIE: Come on, then.

[*Pause.*]

JINTY: Are you ready to go now? (Yourself?)

EFFIE: Ach. I'm aye ready.

JINTY: I don't want to rush you.

[*Pause.*]

But I will have to get back.

[*She picks up her bag.*]

EFFIE: Well, Jinty.

JINTY: What, Effie?

EFFIE: I'll have to get back too.

[*She picks up her bag.*]